My Scars Speak

A Journey of Healing, Empowerment, and Purpose Through Pain

Keyerra Williams

BluePrint Publishing: A Division of BlueMuse Inspired, LLC

To all the brave souls carrying scars, both seen and unseen, or for anyone who believes their scars define who they are:

This book honors you, the resilient fighters who face struggles with strength, courage, and grace. Every scar, whether a mark on your skin or a wound in your heart, stands as a testament to your journey and the strength it took to endure. Remember that every scar holds a story, and each story has meaning. You are not limited by what you've gone through, but by how you recover, heal, and flourish afterwards.

I encourage you to remove the bandage and allow God to bring healing. Each of you has a purpose. I wrote this because I once carried many hidden scars, hiding behind a bandage until I reached a point where I couldn't anymore. I had to let go so that God could restore me.

To my husband, Tito, thank you for being my steadfast support, loving me despite my flaws, and reminding me of my worth. And to my miracle baby, Jazz, my heart is filled with gratitude every day for the blessing of being your mother. You are my motivation to turn scars into stories of hope and inspiration. Let us all embrace our fears and find strength in our shared experiences.

Foreword

There are journeys in life that leave visible scars…and then there are journeys that leave invisible ones; deep, hidden, yet no less powerful. My beloved in whom I'm well pleased, my dear sister, Keyerra Williams, knows both.

I have had the greatest blessing of witnessing her growth up close, not only as her brother but as her Pastor at Victory Temple Outreach Center in Kings Mountain, North Carolina. I've seen her endure storms that would have shaken the strongest of hearts, yet she has remained anchored in faith. I've watched her rise, fall, and rise again and do it time and time again.

She is the epitome of perpetual victory with no brakes. Now, with *My Scars Speaks* the world gets to witness what I have always known: her life is a testament to resilience, perseverance, and God's unwavering faithfulness. I remember the message she declared to me on my birthday: "JUST DO IT!" Simple words, yet they carried the weight of a lifetime of encouragement and prophecy. However, they were not meant just for me, they were meant for her too. She listened. She acted. She obeyed and here we are. Her story, her testimony, her book, in full manifestation.

Keyerra, the journey has not been easy. You have endured miscarriage after miscarriage, each loss forming a deep wound, yet you never allowed despair to take root. You clung to God, stayed prudent in his ways, and pressed forward even when the path seemed impossibly dark. Through it all, you embodied the truth of Psalm 34:18: *"The Lord is near to the brokenhearted and saves the crushed in spirit."*

Each devotional day of this book is a reflection of her scars; each one a story of hope, a lesson in faith, and proof that God is faithful even when life is not easy. Her scars speak, not of defeat, but of VICTORY. They are a consistent reminder that every tear, every setback, every trial is part of a greater story of restoration, purpose, and divine timing. The worst is OVER, you are living already NOW!

As you read this book, may you be reminded that faith is not the absence of struggle, but the courage to persevere through it. May you see the depth of her honesty and the radical transformation of her spirit. Be encouraged to remain steadfast, to trust God's timing, and to honor his process in your life. May you embrace the promise of Isaiah 40:31,*"But those who hope in the Lord will renew their strength. They will soar on wings like eagles; they will run and not grow weary, they will walk and not faint."*

Keyerra, your journey inspires me beyond words. Congratulations on this milestone. Your obedience, patience, relentless faith, and courage are an example to all who know you. Your scars, once a source of pain, are now a source of power. They are a light for those still walking through their valleys, a voice for those who feel unheard, and a hope for those who have yet to see the promise fulfilled. I'm encouraged that God can't lie and he won't fail. Every promise indeed, shall come to pass! Thank you for not giving up on God's plan for your life.

This book is more than a testimony, it resounds as a clarion call of victory. A declaration that staying faithful, remaining diligent, and trusting God through every season is well worth it. Seasons change and storms cease.

Your story will flow and flourish beyond borders to touch millions, inspire countless hearts, and remind the world that scars are not marks of failure, they are evidence (God given proof) of resilience, unshakable faith, and the glory of God manifest in a human life. May every page of this book remind readers: Stay faithful. Be prudent. Endure. Trust and always remember, the results of obedience to God are worth every struggle.

To God We Give Praise,

+Overseer-Designate Quintarro T. Smith
Brother, Pastor, & Senior Pastor/Establishmentarian
Victory Temple Outreach Center
Kings Mountain, North Carolina

Preface

Uncovering the Stories Within

Every scar tells a story, serving as proof of the battles we've fought and the journeys we've endured. They are more than marks on our skin; they serve as vivid reminders of our resilience, showcasing our capacity to heal and grow. In this book, "My Scars Speak," I invite you to begin a journey of self-discovery and healing. Together, we will explore the stories behind our scars, both visible and those that are invisible.

This book aims to showcase the beauty and strength that come from our imperfections. Life is filled with challenges that leave their mark on us, but it is through these experiences that we discover purpose and define who we are. Embracing our scars is an act of bravery and empowerment, enabling us to turn pain into wisdom.

In an era when vulnerability is often mistaken for weakness, I want to challenge that notion. Our scars can act as bridges, connecting us to our true selves and others. While others have shared similar struggles that reveal their scars, I aim to show that we're not alone; each scar tells a story that is uniquely ours but also universally relatable.

As you flip through this book, I encourage you to reflect on your scars and the experiences that have shaped you. Reflect on what they have taught you and how they have contributed to your growth. Accepting our scars involves allowing the light of healing to shine through and understanding that we are shaped not by our wounds but by our resilience and capacity to rise after every fall.

This book celebrates our capacity to heal and underscores the significance of community in our journeys. You're invited to shed shame and fear, letting your scars tell their stories and lead you toward a brighter, more authentic future. Each person has a purpose and a story worth sharing, and I hope this book serves as a space for reflection, healing, and empowerment.Let's begin this journey together, exploring the stories and secrets beneath the surface and honoring the beauty of the scars that define us.

For example, my inner scars from losing a child symbolize life amid loss and emptiness. My surgical scars stand for survival and serve as a reminder that things could have been different. Each of you has scars that reflect personal experiences, reminding you of the pain, the loss, and those difficult moments when it felt like it was just too overwhelming.

Furthermore, the story behind my scars shows my endurance, faith, and the many prayers God answered. This brought me peace, healing, and restoration. Nothing compares to feeling at peace and complete in your life, embracing everything God has blessed you with. Now, I can live freely and fully.

My husband and I met through one of his cousins. At that time, I was emotionally exhausted and struggling with life's challenges, not even considering marriage or love. He had tried to reach out to me before, but I didn't notice. This makes me realize that what we often think we don't want might be what we need. I'm grateful that our paths crossed and brought us together, allowing us to fall in love. Little did I know that my friendship with Tito would change my life forever and lead us to this moment.

When I was younger, I always dreamed of being part of a big family; just the thought of creating love and memories with my own family excited me. Growing up, you often saw two-parent households, but they weren't always families working together as one.

Sometimes, you see one parent managing the household while the other chooses when to be involved or stay absent. Maybe you can relate because you had the picture of two parents inside your home, but not the connection, or maybe your household was a single-parent home, where one parent did everything to keep things running smoothly.

In either case, we all have come to some conclusions about how we desire our family to be. While the best case scenario is to have a two-parent household, we know this is not always the model for everyone. However, we also must realize, that not being raised with both parents who are working together effectively in the home has challenged how many of us were raised and how we show up in our everyday life.

As a result, of my family model, I remember saying I would be a present parent and build a legacy for my family. I always believed that the cycle would end with me because I didn't want my children to feel unloved; I wanted them to know that I loved them and that I was always there for them.

I believe God has a purpose for me because even during times when I felt alone, I would write about my day in a journal, attach a happy picture, or reflect on how I could respond differently in certain situations. In conclusion, as we deal with those who are broken because of the absence of fathers leading, we can't continue to negate how this has impacted so many and how that narrative should change.

I wrote this book with the intention of sharing my story, but also to help you deal with how your story is valuable and healing is available. You can read this book continuously or use it as a devotional, a guide used to reflect upon your personal healing journey. However, you decide to do that is up to you…but by all means, allow it to be a source of healing for your soul.

Introduction

Wombs (The Genesis of Scars)

Every journey begins in the sanctuary of the womb, where life starts and the earliest echoes of our existence resound. This space is more than just a physical vessel; it reflects potential, vulnerability, and many hidden struggles. In this early stage, we unknowingly encounter the initial scars that will shape our lives.

Just as my scars tell a story of endurance, so do the invisible marks we inherit from previous generations. While wrapped in warmth and security, we are also subtly influenced by the outside world. Our mothers' experiences; her joys, fears, and struggles can leave us with invisible yet powerful impressions even before we are born. Research shows that a mother's stress and trauma during pregnancy can significantly impact fetal development, leaving emotional legacies that shape how we respond to life long before we are born. These early experiences establish the foundation of our identity, shaping how we perceive love, safety, and trust. So let's start by exploring the profound significance of these initial moments and their impact on our perspective of the world and ourselves.

I'll share personal stories from my life, reflecting on how the experiences I've had since before birth have shaped patterns that are evident throughout my journey. What once felt like a burden has transformed into a source of strength and resilience. It's essential to recognize that even the most challenging beginnings can lay the groundwork for healing and empowerment. We also need to consider the concept of generational scars and the emotional and psychological wounds passed down through families. These scars develop over time and influence our mental and emotional well-being. By examining this complex pattern, we can identify common themes in our lives, helping us understand the legacies we carry and the stories we have the power to change.

As we go through this devotional together and this day specifically...I encourage you to reflect deeply on your roots. What emotional wounds might have formed from your earliest memories? What lessons have these wounds taught you, and how have they shaped your sense of self and your relationships with others? Recognizing these roots isn't just about reflection; it's a necessary step toward healing and a fundamental foundation for accepting the very wounds that shape us. The womb may genuinely be the source of our scars, but it is also the birthplace of hope and transformation. By embracing our stories, we can honor the remarkable strength that comes from our beginnings. Just as a seed must crack open to grow, we too can rise from our scars, guided by the wisdom of our roots and empowered to thrive.

In conclusion, let's recognize that our scars those that are both visible and hidden. Because they tell stories of resilience rooted in our earliest moments. Together, let's honor these origins as we embark on a transformative journey of healing and self-discovery, understanding that each scar has a purpose and lessons to guide us forward. Life often compels us to confront our past, present, and future directly. In these moments, our human nature tends to resist facing everything that has occurred because revisiting memories, recalling circumstances, and seeing faces can be overwhelming. However, if we recognize that our scars are vital parts of our healing and proof that we've survived what we thought would break us, we can generally handle everything we've been through more effectively.

Scars come from moments of deep vulnerability when we are hurt, injured, or broken. They can be physical, resulting from accidents, surgeries, or illnesses. They can also be emotional, stemming from heartbreak, loss, or trauma. Each scar, regardless of its cause, tells a unique story and it is a part of our personal history that can teach, transform, and heal us. The key is to learn from what our scars represent. We should not let those scars paralyze us or prevent us from moving forward. What experiences in your life have made you feel stuck because you've let them define your future? When was the last time you reflected on your story and its role in your life? A scar in my life has taught me a deep lesson and brought healing.

On August 26, 2006, I welcomed my beautiful angel, Kamayah. Carrying a child for nine months only to lose her immediately after birth was heartbreaking. I remember hearing her first cry, then silence. The pain and frustration stayed, and I felt robbed of the joy of motherhood. I recall lying in the hospital bed, the monitors beeping like a countdown of my fears. My body felt strange, my mind hurried, and a heavy silence filled the room. That moment started a journey I didn't choose but one that would change me forever.

Despite experiencing pain and setbacks, I found a sense of purpose in my loss. I wanted my child, but I believe that God needed her more. I prayed for her, envisioned her, and made plans for her life. However, suddenly, it all seemed to slip away from my grasp. Grief has a way of infiltrating every part of your being. It affects more than just your emotions; it settles into your mind, body, and even in small moments you never expected to be painful, like walking past the baby aisle in the store or hearing someone casually mention your child's name. Some of you may be struggling not only with grief but also with guilt, shame, and the quiet question many mothers carry: Was it my fault? That question can occupy your mind for too long. While others may have moved on, you might be stuck in the moment, replaying it over and over, hoping for a different outcome that will never come.

But God is the one who can transform everything and help you live again. You might not be asking for a miracle to undo the pain or for the strength to endure it. But gradually, He will guide you through the healing process, not around it, not skipping past it, but through it without rushing. He met me in my tears, silence, doubts, and even anger. And in that valley, I learned something powerful: healing does not erase the scar; it gives it purpose. As briefly as it was, my daughter's life changed mine forever. And although I didn't get to raise her, she inspired in me a more profound sense of compassion, a stronger purpose, and a calling to help others through their pain. It took years, but I began to see beauty emerge from the ashes of what I once thought would destroy me.

Have you ever experienced a moment when you felt lost because of a traumatic event? Then you probably understand the pain and confusion I went through. Moments like these, if not handled carefully, can make or break us. I don't know your story, but I do know that if you've faced any hardship, what didn't kill you has helped strengthen you. We often don't realize how strong and resilient we are until we face trials and challenges that test us, eventually revealing our inner strength and areas where we're stronger than we thought. Our resilience shines through in the face of significant challenges, fear, and frustration.

While our scars may remain, they do not define us; instead, they serve as reminders not of defeat or shame but of survival.

They show that even when life tried to break us, we endured. We bent, but we didn't break. And somehow, by God's grace, we kept going. My story might be different from yours, but the connection between us is that we made it. And if you're still here, your purpose is still alive. Take a moment to reflect on your scars. What are they still trying to tell you? What have they taught you about yourself, your faith, and your calling? Do whatever it takes! Even if it means you have to write your own scar story, pray for healing, or share your testimony with someone else. You owe it to yourself to understand the scars that have come to define you so you can reshape how you see the role they played in your life.

Scripture:

For you, I was created; you knit me together in my mother's womb. I praise you because I am fearfully and wonderfully made; your works are wonderful; I know that full well.

Psalm 139:13-14(NIV)

Reflection/Journal:

What scar in my life has shaped who I am today?" How did it influence my faith?

How can I see this scar as a source of strength rather than shame?

Daily Affirmations:

I declare that my beginning does not determine my ending but God does.

Even in broken places, God is creating beauty through me.

My scars aren't something to be ashamed of; they
serve as proof of God's hand in my life.

I honor my womb and the stories it carries.
I acknowledge every scar, whether visible
or hidden, as part of my journey.
I celebrate my strength, resilience, and the healing within me.

I am deserving of love, joy, and peace. My past does not
define me; it directs me toward a brighter future.

I let go of any shame or fear linked to my scars, standing
confidently in my truth as a uniquely beautiful being.

Release Prayer:

I release the burdens of pain, loss, and sorrow tied to my womb.
I let go of the fear and shame around my scars, knowing they are
not a sign of defeat but a testament to my survival and growth.

I invite healing into my life, allowing love and light to
wash over my past wounds. I surrender my fears to God,
trusting that I am whole, cherished, and purposefully
made. I am free to embrace new beginnings, stepping
into my power with grace and confidence.

Day One

Hidden Battles - Don't Let Your Diagnosis Define Your Future

When we consider our stories. often there are invisible struggles many people face, especially those with diagnoses that can overshadow their identity and potential. I am concerned about how these hidden battles can manifest in different forms, such as mental health issues, chronic illness, or societal expectations. Physical scars are the most visible, often serving as symbols of resilience.

They are the remnants of battles fought and won, injuries endured and overcome. Consider the scar from a surgical procedure, the result of a life-saving intervention that marks a turning point in someone's health journey, or the wounds from an accident, reminders of a day that changed everything in an instant. These scars can become symbols of strength, badges of honor worn proudly. They tell us that we survived and are still here despite the challenges. They can also be sources of insecurity, reminders of pain and fear we might want to forget. However, by recognizing and embracing these scars, we find the courage to face our vulnerabilities and celebrate our healing.

Understanding the Diagnosis:

I remember the moment I was diagnosed with stage 4 endometriosis in 2020, and I couldn't get my head around it. I kept asking myself, "What is endometriosis, and how did I end up here?" My menstrual cycles were a nightmare, filled with excruciating pain and heavy bleeding that made me feel like I needed the biggest pads they had, which honestly looked like diapers. I chuckled a little at that absurdity, but it was also terrifying. There were times I passed out or had to take days off work to lie in bed.

After one terrible episode, I rushed to my OB-GYN, desperate for answers, convinced that something had to give. However, when I arrived, the doctor informed me that he couldn't do anything further. I had tried different birth control methods over the years, but they hadn't worked, so he referred me to a pelvic specialist. That appointment was a whirlwind of assessments: they asked about my menstrual cycle, bowel movements, and finally performed a pelvic exam. An ultrasound was done to look for cysts, though I learned it might not always detect early-stage endometriosis. The journey ended with a laparoscopy, a minimally invasive surgery where they made small incisions to examine my pelvic area.

When my doctor finally gave me the news, "Mrs. Williams, you have stage 4 endometriosis", my world felt like it shrank to a bubble. I was in shock, and although he explained that there were treatment options available to manage my pain, there is no cure. After hearing that, I remember zoning out afterward. Deep down, my faith told me that God could turn this around, and that gave me the calm I needed to discuss ways to handle my symptoms. We decided to try a medication that would stop my period altogether, but I had to deal with side effects like hot flashes and anxiety. So, I started taking Orilissa pills every day, and honestly, I prayed over each one before swallowing, hoping for relief.

The truth is, though, it was a tough road. I started losing my hair, which made me feel insecure and unrecognizable. I avoided taking pictures with my family because I was so self-conscious about my appearance. I hid my struggles from my child, but as my symptoms worsened and my hair continued to fall out, I knew I had to make a change. That's when I decided to start wearing wigs. My mom joined me on that journey, and it was meaningful to have her support as we picked out wigs together. Despite those small victories, things got tough, and I was in the hospital every month. The staff started recognizing me by name, which indicated how serious the situation had become.

One day, my child found me collapsing on the floor, and I was grateful she knew what to do. Eventually, my doctor recommended surgery to relieve my pain. Still, he was hesitant to consider a hysterectomy because of my age and the overall health of my ovaries and fallopian tubes. So, surgery was scheduled, and they found endometriosis inside my uterus, outside my uterus, on my bowels, and affecting my appendix.

Then in 2023, I underwent major stomach surgery where they accessed my abdomen, burned away much of the endometriosis to try and stop its progression, and removed my appendix. They also removed a bowel obstruction. The surgery was successful, but after some time, I started experiencing pain again, along with spasms in my right leg and lower back. Here I go again, taking medication to function and get out of bed. I kept returning to the hospital, where they only gave me steroids and muscle relaxers but they were still not addressing the root problem. I'm still being treated with temporary fixes. From heating pads to ice packs, nothing seems to work, and I begin to cry out to God because I am overwhelmed and confused. I thought I was healed at that moment because I wasn't feeling any more stomach pain.

Later, I learned that endometriosis could spread anywhere in your body, and it had started spreading outside my tissue walls onto the nervous system of my spinal cord and vertebrae. Endometriosis started affecting my mobility, causing difficulty walking on my right leg, with pain extending down the right side of my body. There were weeks when walking was painful. I started physical therapy for my back and leg, including spinal injections. My physical therapist advised me to stop working because my job wasn't helping me heal. She told me the more pressure I put on it, the less likely I was to recover. I felt frustrated because I didn't want to stop working or dancing, especially since I owned a dance studio.

My condition sometimes made it impossible to dance, which frustrated me because dance is my life. I remember praying, "Lord, help me because if I can't dance anymore, I don't know what I will do." My husband stood by me through everything and stayed very encouraging, saying God would provide, because little did I know I would have to close my business and stop working. That only added to my frustration, as being on bed rest, going to physical therapy, and being limited in wearing heels made everything worse.

I reached out to my pelvic specialist for a second opinion. During that visit, I went in hoping he'd say something different, but after reviewing my scans and tests, he told me he felt like a hysterectomy was necessary. He explained it was the best option because once endometrial tissue spreads, that's the only way to relieve pressure on my spine. He also said the surgery would prevent me from having more children. When I asked if there were alternatives, he noted hysterectomy was the only practical solution.

Tears started to fall as I realized I had already decided to go ahead with the first surgery, thinking it would improve my situation and give me a chance to have another child later. After careful thought, I decided to proceed. The date was set, and I prepared myself. But I will be honest, every day I was second-guessing myself, as if to say, 'God, I know you are a healer, and I know it's not too late for you to do it for me.' One day at church, I heard my pastor, Quintarro Smith, say, "Do not let your diagnosis be your destiny," which struck a deep chord in me.

I realized I needed to activate my faith and trust in the Lord's report. Even though I prayed, fasted, and believed, I admit I felt frustrated and overwhelmed at times because the healing hadn't happened yet. However, I understand that such feelings are a natural part of the faith journey and need to be navigated. I chose to trust God and canceled my surgery, deciding to walk in my healing as if it were already complete. That was when the scars on my stomach no longer bothered me. Yes, they are still there, but they no longer hold me back.

The Heavy Burden of Stigma

In our society, specific diagnoses, whether mental health conditions, chronic illnesses, or developmental challenges, are often met with stigma that can profoundly impact those affected. This stigma can cause feelings of isolation and misunderstanding, creating a gap between individuals and the support they need. Many people with these diagnoses might hesitate to share their experiences out of fear of judgment or ridicule, which only worsens the loneliness linked to their conditions.

Stereotypes about different diagnoses can be harmful and misleading. For example, someone with anxiety might be viewed as overly sensitive or weak, while people with depression could be called "lazy" or "unmotivated." These broad stereotypes ignore the complexities of their experiences, reducing them to a single story. Such views not only cause misunderstanding but also make people more likely to stay silent as they face both their condition and societal judgment.

To combat this stigma, it's essential to promote compassion and understanding. Recognizing that each person's journey is unique can help eliminate stereotypes that perpetuate stigma. By listening to and affirming the experiences of those facing these hidden challenges, we can build a more inclusive community. Instead of jumping to conclusions, we should ask questions and offer support, thereby creating a safe space for open and honest conversations.Furthermore, education plays a crucial role in reducing stigma. By raising awareness about various diagnoses, we can dispel misconceptions and foster a better understanding.

When society recognizes that these conditions are often beyond a person's control and that seeking help demonstrates strength rather than weakness, it promotes healing and connection. By cultivating a culture of empathy, we can illuminate the darkness of stigma. Every act of kindness and understanding can have a profound impact on someone's life. It's vital to remember that everyone bears their burdens, and through compassion, we not only support others but also enrich our own lives. Ultimately, our shared humanity unites us, reminding us that we are stronger together in the fight against stigma.

Personal Resilience:

For example, my child needed emergency surgery this year after an 11cm ovarian cyst was discovered, leaving scars from the procedure. I recall my child asking, 'Mom, will I have to go through what you did? Will I be in and out of the hospital?' I confidently replied, 'No, the cycle is broken,' meaning every word. Still, inwardly, I felt like crying because my child saw my pain and understood what I had endured. Her eyes showed worry, and her tone shifted as she asked what was next. Yet I refused to let her think, 'I'm going to get endometriosis too.' I took steps to educate myself further and continued to attend doctor visits.

Reclaiming Identity:

It's important to remember that your diagnosis is just one

part of who you are. Start by thinking about your passions and interests beyond your condition. Engage in activities that bring you happiness and purpose, whether it's art, writing, sports, or volunteering. Surround yourself with supportive people who lift your spirits and inspire you to find new ways to express yourself. Consider journaling to track your journey, focusing not just on challenges but also on celebrating your accomplishments, no matter how small. This practice can help you redefine your identity beyond the medical label. Trust me, it was my prayers to God and my support team that kept me fighting and moving forward. I also wrote down and recorded videos of every moment to see how I managed to get through a bad day.

Encouragement to Embrace Life Beyond Struggles and Limitations

Remember, you are more than your challenges. You are created in His image, which means you are more powerful than any situation. Create a vision board that showcases your dreams, goals, and what makes you unique. Each day, take small steps toward those aspirations, understanding that progress can be slow. Embrace the parts of your life that bring you happiness and fulfillment, all of the relationships, hobbies, and experiences that make you feel alive. Declarations can also be helpful; remind yourself daily that you are capable, whole, and deserving of a life filled with hope and purpose. By focusing on these positive aspects, you empower yourself to live authentically and fully embrace your identity, unaffected by any limitations.

Empowering Mindset Shifts:

- You are not the victim of your diagnosis; you didn't cause it. I emphasize this because we often wonder if we are responsible for what happened or why it's happening to us. Seek practical advice for shifting your mindset from victimhood to one of empowerment and hope.

- Writing down techniques for setting and reaching personal goals, despite challenges, will also shift your mindset because you're setting the standard.

- Building connections with others who share similar experiences is essential for creating a support system that fosters understanding and encouragement.

- I remember joining a Facebook community for endometriosis where people shared their stories. The support I received from the group made a difference in my journey. I had people who understood what I was going through, and I heard about different experiences that affected them. I also recall browsing Instagram and reading stories about Tia Mowry and the singer Monica. I believe more people have had to face this terrible disease.

But there is help for you and God is there to help you through the hard places. So as you meditate, reflect and journal today may His help strengthen you in whatever journey you are facing.

Scripture:

"For I know the plans I have for you," declares the Lord, "plans to prosper you and not to harm you, plans to give you hope and a future." Jeremiah 29:11 (NIV)

Reflection/Journal:

What hidden battles have I faced silently?

How can I redefine my story beyond the struggle?

Affirmations:

I declare that nothing hidden is wasted
but God is working even in silence.

I walk in victory over battles no one sees,
because God sees me. My secret struggles
are turning into public testimonies.

I am more than my circumstances. I embrace my
journey and trust that I am being guided toward
a future filled with hope and purpose.

My challenges do not define me; they are simply stepping
stones on my path to strength and resilience. I choose to
rise above and create a beautiful life full of possibilities.

Release Prayer:

Dear God, I come to You today with a heart full of
burdens from the hidden battles I face.

I release to you the fears, doubts, and labels that have been
placed upon me. I ask for your strength to overcome every
diagnosis and trial, knowing that they do not define my future.

Fill me with Your peace and guide me toward the
purpose You have designed for my life.

Help me let go of what weighs me down and
embrace the hope and promise of tomorrow.

Thank you for walking with me every step of the way, and for the healing and restoration that are on the horizon.

I know that with you by my side that whatever may come my way that I am not alone. I realize that even in every obstacle I face that it is an opportunity to see you perform miracles right in the midst of it.

I believe your will is being performed in my life and for that I give you praise! In Your holy name, I pray. Amen.

Day Two

Hiding Behind the Scar (Emotional Scars: The Silent Impact)

Emotional scars, though unseen, are just as pronounced as physical ones. These scars originate from life's most painful experiences of loss, betrayal, rejection, and grief. They shape our perceptions, influence our relationships, and impact our mental health. The pain carried by these scars can be overwhelming, often lasting long after the initial wound has healed. However, emotional scars can also lead to meaningful growth, teaching us empathy, resilience, and self-care. By processing and understanding the pain, we can better face life's challenges with wisdom and compassion. Sharing our emotional scars through stories and conversations can be a powerful way to connect, helping others realize they are not alone in their struggles.

Reflecting on those silent scars, you realize how much you hide or mask inside because you don't want others to see the real you. When I think about a moment when I hid my emotional pain from others, I think about people I once considered friends who secretly undermined me and those I would go out of my way for, yet they caused me pain. The ones I always show up for were nowhere to be found when I needed them. Sometimes, I felt like an outsider within my own family. But I brushed it off and continued to love unconditionally because the value of family means so much to me. Think about it...when family doesn't act like family, have you ever felt these emotions or wondered if others truly see you?

So for many of you, have you stopped to explore how managing your parents' struggles have shaped and informed you. If so, in many cases, it may have made it harder to recognize what a normal living environment is. These behaviors may distort your sense of reality, and cause it to be harder to have the strength to break free from these influences, including breaking generational curses. It means stepping into unknown territory with the awareness that you want something different. You seek change because you've given so much of yourself. People often overlook how certain experiences, especially with those they love, affect their emotions. Take a moment to think about how you see yourself as powerless or purposeless, or even less anointed when others judge you by appearances or undervalue you, as if who you are doesn't matter. That's the time to remember that you were called too, and you also have a purpose. Those are things that can becomes scars to us, and no matter what kind of scar you face, God is able to heal them all.

Scripture:

"My grace is sufficient for you, for my power is made perfect in weakness." 2 Corinthians 12:9

Reflection/Journal:

How has hiding my pain impacted my relationships?

How can I reveal my authentic self?

Affirmations:

I no longer hide. I shine with the
light of Christ within me.

I declare that my scars are not weaknesses
but proof of God's grace.

Shame has no authority over me;
I stand boldly in truth.

I acknowledge my emotional scars as part of my journey, but they do not define me. I am healing, growing, and becoming stronger every day.

I embrace the love and support around me and choose to let go of past pain, allowing joy and hope to fill my heart.

Release Prayer:

Dear God, I come to You with emotional scars weighing heavily on my heart. I release the hurt, sadness, and burdens I have been carrying.

Please grant me the strength to heal from these past wounds and find peace on my journey. Help me see my scars not as signs of pain, but as symbols of resilience and growth.

Fill me with Your love and peace, guiding me toward a future where I can embrace joy and connection without fear.

I release all fear of the future because I realize that you have not given me the spirit of fear, but rather you have given me the spirit of love, power, and a sound mind.

So I acknowledge my scars but I will not allow them to

cause me to stay connected to the hurt or pain of the past. I will not allow them to cause my mind to stay connected to trauma that I've released and pain I've been healed from.

Thank you for your healing touch and for being with me every step of the way. In your love, I find hope. Amen.

Day Three

Warfare (Navigating Relationships and Emotional Turmoil)

Relationships are the battleground where many of our emotional scars form. The pain inflicted by those we care about can be some of the deepest, leaving lasting marks on our minds. The emotional rollercoaster of managing relationships with family, friends, or partners often feels like an endless war. Each betrayal, rejection, and misunderstanding adds to this hidden conflict, leaving us to cope with its effects. In these turbulent times, our emotional scars stand as quiet witnesses to our struggles. They hold memories of nights when we questioned our worth, echoes of harsh words that linger long after being spoken, and shadows of broken promises. These scars remind us of the vulnerability we felt, the trust we gave, and the pain we endured. Yet, they also reflect our resilience and strength to get back up after each fall. They represent the courage to keep moving forward despite the wounds.

Addressing conflicts in relationships means confronting these wounds directly. It requires us to examine our feelings deeply, identify the roots of our pain, and work toward healing. This can involve setting boundaries to protect ourselves, breaking ties with toxic people, or finding ways to rebuild trust where it has been broken. It is a journey of self-discovery and empowerment, where we learn to prioritize our well-being and recognize our core values.

Sharing our stories of emotional struggles can be a powerful act of solidarity and a means of healing. By sharing our experiences, we create a space for others to do the same, fostering a sense of community and mutual support. These conversations can help us realize that we are not alone in our struggles and that there is strength in vulnerability. Ultimately, our emotional scars are more than just reminders of pain, they serve as proof of our survival, growth, and capacity for empathy. They teach us to be kinder to ourselves and others, to value the lessons from our struggles, and to accept the healing process. As we navigate the highs and lows of relationships, we come to realize that our scars have much to communicate, and through them, we can discover a path to wholeness and peace.

Sometimes, we have been in so much trauma that we misunderstand how to be loved properly, so we stay in relationships we should exit. As a result, we will stay engaged in places due to the fear of being alone. Have you ever felt lonely or not chosen? Loving someone who doesn't return your feelings is like taking refuge in the idea of "love." You convince yourself they're the one, pouring your heart into the relationship even as you feel unappreciated.you Then they reveal who they truly are, but you choose to ignore the signs yes, all the signs right there before you. Remember the saying, "When they show you who they are, believe them."

hRelationships can be complicated, leading people to wonder whether to stay or go, hoping for change. Maybe I will stay because I love them and feel I can't do better without them, the thought of being alone or seeking validation from having someone in my life. I hide my true feelings with artificial smiles, matching clothes, and curated social media images to show everyone that this is my man and I'm sticking with him. He showers me with material things, yet he continues to do his own thing, which makes me question his actions.

But, when you know he has other things going on, you've

got to face what's real. The thoughts in my mind are no longer just thoughts; they are realities I don't want to face. Still, I find the strength to move forward, only to end up with the same treatment in my next relationship, just with a different face. Why? Because I never gave myself time to heal from the first one. Just thinking about it leaves me feeling empty; no one is filling my cup again because I look for love in the wrong places, getting the bare minimum which looks like, no affection, no response, no care. I'm losing sleep and losing myself, and they don't even care; it doesn't bother them how I feel. I'm screaming inside. Do they see me? The warfare in your mind is intense, but it can still be brought to an end.

Yes, so you can pray and pray, but still feel the same, and no progress happens. Let's peel back one more layer. The inner war comes from wrestling with yourself because you don't realize your value or worth. Stop ignoring the signs. You already know what to do. Just go on and everything will be okay. Take that step. We're about to move forward.

Scripture:

Do not be anxious about anything, but in every situation, through prayer and petition, with thanksgiving, present your requests to God. And the peace of God, which surpasses all understanding, will guard your hearts and your minds in Christ Jesus. Philippians 4:6-7 (NIV)

Affirmation:

I am resilient in the face of emotional turmoil and relationship challenges.

I trust that God is guiding me through every storm. I release my fears and anxieties, embracing peace and clarity in my heart.

I am worthy of healthy relationships,
and I choose to approach my interactions
with love, wisdom, and grace.

Release Prayer:

Dear God, I come to You now, seeking Your strength as I navigate the turbulent waters of relationships and emotional turmoil.

I release my burdens, fears, and the pain that has weighed heavily on my heart.

Help me develop healthy connections and find peace amidst chaos.

Please grant me the wisdom to discern which relationships uplift me and which may be causing harm.

Fill me with Your healing presence and guide me to surround myself with people who reflect Your love and support.

Thank you for your constant guidance and the restoration ahead. In Your name, I pray. Amen.

Day Four

Love Conquers All

As I reflect on this devotion; Love Conquers All, I think about the love between a father and daughter. When I was younger, I was daddy's girl, and I loved my dad. I would spend time with him doing all the typical father-daughter activities. I could feel my dad loved me because his actions and words demonstrated it. Until one day, my father's actions caused him to become filled with anger and rage. A conflict and a bad decision changed our household, and we grew further apart.

My parents' divorce strained my relationship with my dad, to the point where we only stayed in touch once a year or once in a blue moon. I will be honest; it affected me a lot because I wanted my dad in my life. I wanted a bond. I wanted my father around. As I got older, I started to draw my love from God as my Father because I felt the void and emptiness. I remember getting married and struggling because I wanted my dad to walk me down the aisle, but it didn't happen.

It was another hopeful moment, hoping he would show up, but my brother ended up walking me down the aisle. Over the years, I asked God to help me with this challenge and to teach me how to love unconditionally and to heal so I could live without pain. Listen, God did it. He healed my broken heart. He allowed my father and me to reunite, have a conversation, and release everything that was on our hearts.

I was able to walk away free from the hurt, understanding that he can't be that father figure to me until he is healed himself. I respect him for admitting that he can't lead if he's not whole. I will say this: a little girl and grown women need their fathers in their lives. I believe your father is the one who models and shows you how you should be loved and valued.

Love, at its purest, can heal even the deepest wounds. It is the balm that soothes our souls and the force that keeps us united. When we choose to love, we create space for healing, not only for ourselves but also for those around us. Love teaches us to be compassionate, understanding, and forgiving qualities essential for handling the emotional challenges of relationships. It's important to know that as we navigate life, love becomes our guiding light, helping us see beyond the scars and appreciate the beauty in everyone we meet. It encourages us to extend grace to ourselves and others, understanding that everyone faces their struggles. By loving unconditionally, we create a space where healing can happen, wounds can be mended, and hearts can be restored.

In our emotional battles, love cures pain and suffering. It helps us break down walls built by hurt and betrayal and rebuild trust and connection. Love gives us the strength to forgive those who have wronged us, to let go of bitterness that holds us back, and to embrace the possibility of a brighter, more harmonious future. Love also demands vulnerability and the willingness to open our hearts despite the risk of getting hurt. It is through this vulnerability that genuine healing happens. When we allow ourselves to be seen and to see others, we form a bond that goes beyond scars and reflects our shared humanity. This mutual recognition and acceptance set the stage for healing, helping us move forward with courage and hope.

Love conquers all because it changes us on the deepest level. It shifts how we see things, softens even the hardest hearts, and pushes us to act with kindness and understanding. As we learn to love ourselves and others, we discover the powerful healing ability of love and how it can bring completeness to our lives. As you reflect on your scars, remember that love is the key to your healing journey. Let love guide, strengthen, and transform you. Through love, you can navigate the complexities of relationships and find peace amid emotional turmoil. Embrace love, and watch it conquer all, leading you toward healing and harmony.

So, with love conquers all, I remember asking this question: How do you respond in love when people try to overlook you in certain ways? My great-grandmother would say that you overlook them with love, and you love them the way Jesus loves them. I would ask, but how, when you know how they feel about you and how they have treated you? She would respond so gracefully, baby, you still love them like God loves them. It is the wisdom she left me that keeps me loving those despite how I feel. The song that always comes to mind as a reminder is the love of Jesus.

Scripture:

And now, these three endure: faith, hope, and love. But the greatest of these is love. 1 Corinthians 13:13 (NIV)

Reflection/Journal:

How has love transformed a difficult situation?
How can I actively practice love daily?

Affirmations:

I declare that perfect love casts out fear.
Love is my weapon, and I choose it daily.
God's love heals every wound and covers every scar.

I embrace love as the transformative force in my life. I believe in love's power to heal wounds, mend relationships, and bring joy to my heart.

I choose to love unconditionally, opening my heart to the beauty and connection that surrounds me.

I am worthy of deep and meaningful love, and I attract relationships that uplift and inspire me.

Release Prayer:

Dear God, I come to You with a heart open to love and healing. I release any past hurts, bitterness, or fear that have held me back from experiencing the fullness of love.

Help me recognize the love that exists within and around me, and guide me in showing that love to others.

Give me the courage to be vulnerable and trust in the love that can transform my life.

Fill me with Your light and help me become an instrument of Your love.

Thank you for your endless grace and the healing that comes through love.

In Your holy name, I pray. Amen.

Day Five

The Process of Saying Yes (The Healing Journey)

In reflecting on these truths, it becomes clear that the journey of healing is not only about mending what is broken, but about responding to adversity with an open and loving heart. Love, in its purest form, is a conscious choice and a decision to rise above pain, misunderstandings, and wounds inflicted by others. My great-grandmother's wisdom echoes through the years: to love others, even when they overlook or mistreat you, is to mirror the boundless love that God pours into us. This is neither easy nor natural, especially when your heart remembers every slight and every cold shoulder. Yet, choosing love becomes the very foundation upon which true healing is built. It is both an act of courage and of faith.

As we embark on our healing journeys, we must acknowledge that love alone does not erase the scars, but it does transform how we carry them. For physical scars, this may include seeking medical treatment, engaging in physical therapy, or adopting a lifestyle that promotes health and recovery. For emotional wounds, healing often involves therapeutic methods such as counseling, mindfulness, and creative activities and spaces where acceptance and compassion can flourish. Spiritual healing, on the other hand, may include practices such as fasting, prayer, and forming authentic connections with others who support your growth.

As we explore what it truly means to say 'yes" know that it

is a call to healing, to love, and to what rests on your spirit. I remember the moment I told God, "Yes." That single word was the threshold between fear and faith, and it marked the beginning of a new chapter in my ministry. Saying yes is rarely easy. Often, it means stepping into the unknown, trusting the blueprint God reveals, even when you must build each step with trembling hands. There are times when you may feel isolated, misunderstood, or even rejected by others who cannot see your vision or who doubt your purpose. I recall moments of deep discouragement and searching for a place to plant my Christian dance studio, being turned away by realtor after realtor, feeling that my dream was unwanted. Yet, every closed door became an invitation to persevere; every detour was a test of faith.

Eventually, through persistence and unwavering belief, Elevated Praise Dance Studio opened its doors to the community. It became not just a business, but a ministry; offering hope, creativity, and worship. Though the studio operated for only three years before closing due to health challenges, I do not see this as a defeat. Instead, I recognize it as a chapter in a larger story, a testament to resilience and the willingness to try again. Now, I look forward to reopening with anticipation, armed with the lessons and strength the journey has provided.

Every path to healing, whether physical, emotional, or spiritual requires intention and a sense of grace. You may face setbacks, doubts, or even heartbreak along the way. There will be days when progress feels small and hope seems distant. But remember: every act of self-care, every prayer, every moment you choose compassion over bitterness, is a step toward wholeness. By tending to our wounds and honoring our stories, we build resilience and deepen our spirit, equipping ourselves for life's challenges with greater courage.

Healing is not a straight line. Progress ebbs and flows; clarity and confusion will walk hand in hand. Yet, by embracing love and self-compassion, you lay a solid foundation for lasting transformation. Permit yourself to heal at your own pace. Explore the methods that resonate with you, seek out supportive communities, and trust the wisdom of your body, mind, and spirit. Healing is a personal journey, and your path is unique.

Scripture:

Behold, I will do a new thing; now it will spring forth; will you not recognize it? I will even make my way through the wilderness and across the rivers in the desert.

Isaiah 43:19 (NKJV)

Reflection/Journal:

Where have I resisted healing and growth?

How can I say "yes" to my journey today?

Affirmations:

I declare that my "yes" opens the door to my destiny.
I trust God's plan, even when I can't see the full picture.
My obedience will bring blessings for generations to come.

I embrace love as the transformative force in my life. I believe in love's power to heal wounds, mend relationships, and bring joy to my heart.

I choose to love unconditionally, knowing that I am worthy of deep, meaningful connections and that I attract relationships that uplift and inspire me.

I am open to healing and transformation in my life. I trust the journey ahead and welcome the changes that come my way.

With each step, I release old burdens and create space for new beginnings. I am deserving of love, peace, and joy, and I embrace the blessings unfolding in my life.

Release Prayer:

Dear God, I come to You with a heart open to love and healing. I release any past hurts, bitterness, or fear that have held me back from experiencing the fullness of love.

Help me recognize the love that exists within and around me, and guide me in showing that love to others. Give me the courage to be vulnerable and trust in the love that can transform my life.

Fill me with Your light and help me become an instrument of Your love.

Thank you for your endless grace and the healing that comes through love. In Your holy name, I pray. Amen.

Day Six

Survival Kit (Embracing Our Scars)

Ultimately, our scars are part of who we are. They are a testament to our life journey and resilience. "My Scars Speaks" celebrates the strength and beauty these marks represent. It honors the stories they tell and the lessons they convey. By embracing our scars, we honor our past, recognize our growth, and move forward with courage and grace. This devotional book encourages us to reflect on the scars we carry, both visible and invisible, and to understand how profoundly they impact our lives. Through personal stories, reflections, and insights, readers are encouraged to explore their own experiences, finding comfort and strength in the narratives that their scars represent. In these stories, we see that scars are not just signs of pain but also symbols of survival, resilience, and the human spirit.

I can finally stand tall and shout. I survived days I never thought I would…I made it with tears streaming down my face. I endured when I wanted to quit, and now I feel like there's nothing I can't do. I survived to thrive. I am alive because there's more. Those words carry power, and you might not realize it until you face a life experience where you have to stand by and fight for them.

The survival kit is when you can step out of hiding, take off the mask and look in the mirror at your true self, when you can reflect on the past without pain or tears, and when you can see beauty in the scars from your surgeries instead of just marks on your skin.

The Survival Kit: Uplifting Godly Messages to Embrace Our Scars

1. You Are Fearfully Made:

Embrace your scars as part of who you are. Psalm 139:14 reminds us, "I praise you because I am fearfully and wonderfully made." Your experiences, both joyful and painful, shape your unique story.

2. God's Strength is Made Perfect in Your Weakness:

Remember that His strength is made perfect in your weakness. 2 Corinthians 12:9 states, "My grace is sufficient for you, for my power is made perfect in weakness." Your scars show where His grace shines the brightest.

3. Beauty from Ashes:

God can turn your pain into beauty. Isaiah 61:3 promises us, "to bestow on them a crown of beauty instead of ashes." Trust that He is transforming your trials into a testimony that reflects His glory.

4. You Are Not Alone:

In your struggles and scars, remember that you are never alone. Deuteronomy 31:6 assures us, "The Lord your God goes with you; he will never leave you nor forsake you." Lean on Him for comfort and guidance.

5. Every Scar Tells a Story:

Your scars are a testimony to your journey and resilience. They remind you of battles fought and victories won. Celebrate the story God is telling through your life, because each chapter has a purpose.

6. Trust in God's Plan:

Even when life feels overwhelming, trust that God has a plan for you. Jeremiah 29:11 affirms, "For I know the plans I have for you," declares the Lord, "plans to prosper you and not to harm you." Your scars are part of His greater purpose.

7. Healing Through Forgiveness:

To truly embrace your scars, recognize the power of forgiveness. Ephesians 4:32 encourages us to "forgive each other, just as in Christ God forgave you." Let go of past hurts to experience freedom and healing.

8. Hope in Every Season:

Just as seasons change, so can your circumstances. Lamentations 3:22-23 reminds us, "His mercies are new every morning." Hold onto hope because each new day offers chances for healing and renewal.

9. Walk by Faith:

Your journey is a walk of faith. 2 Corinthians 5:7 tells us, "For we walk by faith, not by sight." Trust in God's promises, even when the path is unclear, knowing He is guiding you toward restoration.

10. Embrace Your Worth:

Remember that you are deeply loved and valued by God. Romans 8:38-39 assures us that nothing can separate us from His love. Your scars do not define you; they are simply part of the beautiful tapestry of who you are in Him.

Embracing your scars means acknowledging your strength

and recognizing the divine craftsmanship within your pain. Trust God's plan for your life, seek healing, and remember that your story is a powerful testament to His unwavering love and grace.

Scripture:

He heals the brokenhearted and binds up their wounds. Psalm 147:3 (NIV)

Reflection/Journal:

What tools or practices have helped me survive challenges?

How can I share these lessons to help others?

Affirmation:

I embrace my scars as symbols of my resilience and strength.

I acknowledge that my past does not define me, and I trust in the healing journey.

Each scar tells a story of survival and growth.

I am worthy of love and light, and I choose to honor my path with grace and compassion.

Release Prayer:

Dear God, thank You for loving me through my scars and struggles. I come to you with an open heart, ready to release the pain and burdens that weigh me down.

Help me see my scars as reminders of my strength and resilience. Please guide me in embracing my past while looking forward to healing and transformation.

Surround me with Your love and grace as
I learn to accept myself completely.

Thank you for the restoration ahead and for filling
my life with hope. In Your holy name, I pray. Amen.

Day Seven

Building a Family Legacy

Building a family legacy is more than passing down possessions; it's about instilling values, traditions, and love that reach across generations. It's a chance to create a foundation that reflects who we are and what we stand for, shaping the lives of those who follow us. To build a legacy, we first need to determine what matters most to us. Which values do we want to pass down to our children? It could be kindness, perseverance, faith, or the importance of education. Our actions often speak louder than words, so we should demonstrate these qualities in our daily lives.

Traditions can be a powerful tool for creating a lasting legacy. They connect us to our heritage and strengthen family bonds. Whether it's a simple family dinner each week, an annual vacation, or special holiday traditions, these shared moments become cherished memories that shape our family identity. These traditions, regardless of size, are the threads that weave our family history and foster a sense of belonging.

Another important aspect is sharing testimonies. Sharing our experiences, struggles, and triumphs helps younger generations understand who they are and where they come from. It gives them a sense of continuity and belonging, reinforcing the idea that they are part of something bigger than themselves. Including stories of resilience, love, and faith in our family narrative empowers them to face their own lives with strength and confidence.

One effective way to build a family legacy is through acts of service. Getting involved in our communities, volunteering, or donating to causes we care about teaches our children the value of giving back. These experiences not only foster empathy but also create a sense of purpose and connection to the world around them.

As we start building a legacy, it's crucial to share our dreams and hopes with our families. Open conversations promote mutual understanding and enable us to support each other in reaching those goals.

Ultimately, building a family legacy is a lifelong commitment. It requires purpose, love, and grace. Challenges will arise, but with consistent effort, we can create a lasting impact on the lives of those we love.

Let's take the opportunity to cultivate a legacy that reflects our values and brings hope, inspiration, and purpose to future generations.

Scripture:

"A good person leaves an inheritance for their children's children…" Proverbs 13:22 (NIV)

Reflection/Journal:

What values do I want to pass on to my family or children?

How can I break generational patterns and create a positive legacy?

Affirmations:

I declare that my family will walk in faith, favor, and freedom.

The cycle of brokenness ends with me. I am dedicated to creating a meaningful family legacy that reflects love, values, and purpose.

With each action, I contribute to building a story that will inspire future generations.

I am grateful for the opportunity to create a legacy.

Release Prayer:

Dear God, thank You for the gift of family and the opportunity to build a legacy of love and purpose. Help me embody values that will guide and inspire my loved ones.

Please grant me the wisdom to nurture meaningful traditions, share our stories, and engage in acts of service.

I release any fears or doubts about my role in this process and trust that you are working through me.

May our family legacy be a source of strength and unity for future generations. In Your name, I pray. Amen.

Day Eight

Coping with Trauma (Finding Peace Amid the Storm)

As I reflect on a traumatic moment in my life, I think about the moments after losing a child, and I must walk back into the environment where my child would have come back to. I remember coming back to my room to see all the baby clothes and everything you needed for your newborn baby filling that space. I remember my mom saying she tried to have everything out before I came because she wanted me to feel at home. I responded with leave it and I just want to be alone. From that moment till it was time to plan my child's funeral, I can recall staying in my room daily just trying to process everything, going days without really wanting to eat and not wanting to interact with anyone. I remember my mom asking me to talk or did I want to talk to someone about how I'm feeling. I responded with "no; I just want to be alone."

So, from the moments of being alone to going to the funeral home to look at caskets, hearing about all the different things that go into burying your child. I remember picking out a casket for my child and just demanding everything to be perfect since it would be the last time I held my child or saw my child.

After the funeral, I remember just releasing everything and crying out to God for help because I wasn't crazy and didn't want to talk to a therapist, I wanted to hear from God, I wanted him to help me. After experiencing that storm in my life, I was able to start removing all my child's clothes, etc., and boxing them for someone in need of baby stuff. In the midst of my hurt, my response was that I wanted to be a blessing to a new mother.

Trauma can feel overwhelming, making us feel lost and alone. However, it's essential to remember that healing is possible and that God walks with us through our darkest moments. This devotional day highlights the importance of coping with trauma by building resilience and finding peace amidst chaos.

God Sees Your Pain:

The Lord understands you're suffering and is there to comfort you. 1 Peter 5:7 encourages us to "Cast all your anxiety on him because he cares for you." He knows your trauma and wants you to find peace in Him.

You Are Stronger Than You Think:

Even when you feel weak, God provides you with the strength you need. Philippians 4:13 reassures us, "I can do all things through him who strengthens me." Trust that you have the resilience to overcome your challenges.

Healing is a Journey:

Healing from trauma takes time. Psalm 34:18 reminds us, "The Lord is close to the brokenhearted and saves those who are crushed in spirit." Give yourself grace during this journey.

Transforming Your Pain:

God can turn your pain into purpose. Romans 8:28 promises, "And we know that in all things God works for the good of those who love him." Trust that your experiences can lead to a greater purpose in your life.

Find Shelter in Him:

During tough times, God is your refuge. Psalm 46:1 says, "God is our refuge and strength, an ever-present help in trouble." Trust Him for support during your moments of crisis.

Renew Your Mind:

God calls you to renew your thoughts and emotions. Romans 12:2 instructs us, "Do not conform to the pattern of this world, but be transformed by the renewing of your mind." Focus on His truth to overcome negative thoughts rooted in trauma.

Surround Yourself with Support:

God places people in our lives to support us. Ecclesiastes 4:9-10 reminds us, "Two are better than one... If either of them falls, one can help the other up." Don't hesitate to ask trusted friends or professionals for help.

You Are Never Alone:

God is always with you, even in the most challenging times. Isaiah 41:10 says, "So do not fear, for I am with you; do not be dismayed, for I am your God." Find comfort in His presence as you work through your healing. Coping with trauma is a complex yet vital process. With God as your guide and source of strength, you can find peace and healing despite life's storms. Embrace the journey and remember that every step forward shows your resilience and faith.

Scripture:

The Lord is close to the brokenhearted. Psalm 34:18

He heals the broken heart and bandages

their wounds. Psalm 147:3 (NIV)

Reflection/Journal:

How do I process trauma?

What steps bring peace?

Affirmations:

I declare that my trauma does not define
me and my triumph does.

God is healing every place of pain, one layer at a time.

I choose peace, restoration, and wholeness in Christ.

I acknowledge my feelings and honor my journey of healing. My trauma does not define me; instead, I am shaped by the strength that arises from it. I trust God's process and embrace the hope of renewal. I am worthy of healing and love, and I choose to move forward with courage.

Release Prayer:

Dear God,

I come before You with a heavy heart, burdened by my trauma.

I thank You for being my comforter and refuge.
Help me release the pain and fear that hold me back
from fully experiencing Your peace and love.

Please guide me on my healing journey and allow
me to see the strength in my struggles.

Help me transform my pain into purpose and surround me with supportive people. I trust in Your plan for my life and lean on Your everlasting promises. In Jesus' name, I pray, Amen.

Day Nine

The Power of Vulnerability

The power of vulnerability, when I think back on a time I risked it, and it led to healing. It was when I made the decision to strengthen my partnership with my husband, not implying we didn't already have a great connection. Still, taking a risk of vulnerability with your spouse by respectfully telling them when they've hurt you, instead of bottling it up inside, is important.

I've always been the kind of person who would hold things in and take them to the Lord in prayer, but in my healing process, it allowed my spouse and me to create a space where we sit down, listen, and don't judge. In those moments, we open up about personal insecurities, such as fears or struggles, which helps us understand each other on a deeper level. When your spouse responds with empathy, it builds trust and emotional intimacy, creating a deeper, more secure bond.

Also, in that moment of opening up and discussing what was on my heart, I discovered I wasn't alone. We both had things that bothered us or hurt us, and it allowed us to be transparent and release it. It also let us reflect on how we could move forward and help each other. Admitting when you need support is the best decision you can make because, by opening up, it allows them to support you, and it creates a closer bond between you.

A time vulnerability cost me is when I made the decision

to live in peace and not in a box with walls built up but it was worth it. For many, the risk is worth it because living an inauthentic life, with walls built up to avoid getting hurt, is more exhausting and less fulfilling. Vulnerability often sparks fear because it requires us to show our true selves to the world. However, in this openness lies great strength. Embracing vulnerability isn't a sign of weakness; instead, it shows courage. It involves being willing to share our stories, struggles, and authentic selves, which helps build connections based on trust and understanding.

When we embrace vulnerability, we reveal the true depth of our humanity. We encourage others to see not just our scars but also our hopes, dreams, and struggles. Sharing in this way can forge meaningful and transformative connections, offering a chance for healing for ourselves and others who relate to our experiences. Vulnerability is also essential in our relationship with God. The Bible encourages us to approach His throne openly and honestly, laying ourselves bare before Him. It's during our moments of weakness that we often experience God's greatest strength. When we drop our defenses, we can more fully receive His love and grace, fostering a deeper and more intimate relationship with our Creator.

Reflect on the teachings of Jesus, who showed vulnerability during his most difficult moments—whether through his honest prayers in the Garden of Gethsemane or his emotional reaction to the death of a friend (John 11:35). His life demonstrates that vulnerability can exist alongside strength, highlighting the beauty of human compassion and connection.

This devotional day invites you to examine your vulnerabilities. What stories are you hiding? What emotions are you afraid to reveal? Recognizing and accepting these feelings can open the door to transformation, helping you move forward with faith and resilience.

Sharing our vulnerabilities, we encourage others to take off their masks. When we share our stories, we remind others that they are not alone in their struggles. We create a safe space for healing and growth, affirming that it's okay to be imperfect and still make progress. As we embrace the power of vulnerability, let's remember that it's in our weaknesses that we often find our greatest strength. It's through our scars that we inspire others to embrace their own stories.

Scripture:

My grace is sufficient for you, because my power is made perfect in weakness.

2 Corinthians 12:9 (NIV)

Reflection/Journal:

How has vulnerability helped me grow?

Where can I practice it now?

Affirmations:

I declare that my openness creates space for healing.

I am safe to be seen, known, and loved.

My vulnerability is not weakness—it is strength wrapped in truth.

I embrace my vulnerability as a source of strength.

I acknowledge that sharing my true self connects
me to others and invites healing.

I am confident that my imperfections do not define me;
instead, they contribute to my unique journey.

I trust in God's grace, which empowers me to
share my story openly and honestly.

Day Ten

Resilience in Adversity

A season in my life where life knocked me down is when I had to stop working because of my health. That season was my hardest season because instead of me going to work every day doing something I loved my new thing was doctor visits, physical therapy three times week and spinal injections every 3-4 weeks. That also included bed rest which consisted of my husband by my side helping me.

Sometimes him doing everything depending on how I felt at the moment. It gave me joy and motivation everytime I saw him taking care of me gracefully not complaining but careful with every detail to make sure his wife and family was taking care of.That was my strength to want to bounce back because my family needed me.

Adversity is an unavoidable part of our human experience. It tests our strength, challenges our beliefs, and often pushes us to our limits. Yet, in these difficult moments, we have a special chance to build our resilience. Resilience isn't just about bouncing back; it's about coming out even stronger and more determined. It's the ability to adapt and succeed despite the storms we face. Life's challenges can seem overwhelming, but each obstacle offers an opportunity to uncover our inner strength. The struggles we face shape us and they teach us about perseverance, patience, and hope. When we accept the discomfort of our situation, we gain a deeper understanding of ourselves and our place in the world.

Overcoming adversity requires a shift in mindset. Instead of viewing struggles as setbacks, we can reflect on the story of the butterfly. Before it emerges in its beautiful form, it must first struggle inside its cocoon. This struggle is essential to its transformation; it is through this fight that the wings grow stronger. Similarly, our struggles often act as catalysts for our personal growth. Facing adversity helps us develop vital skills, including perseverance, empathy, and the ability to inspire others. They are stepping stones to greater resilience. Our scars, whether visible or hidden, symbolize endurance and proof of our journeys. Each scar reminds us of the battles we've fought and the victories we've won.

Resilience looked like defeat at my lowest point, but I viewed the struggle not just as a difficult experience, but as the foundation for growth. I gained a deeper relationship with God, understanding that he is the source of my strength and he was going to see me through. During difficult times, we can turn to Scripture to remind us of God's promises and his constant support. We're not alone in our struggles; He walks with us through every challenge, guiding and uplifting us. This reassurance strengthens our resilience and brings peace to our hearts.

Scripture:

Trials produce perseverance

James 1:2-4

Those who wait on the lord shall renew their strength.

Isaiah 40:31

Reflection/Journal:

"How has adversity shaped me instead of breaking me?"

Affirmations:

I declare that I rise every time I fall.

The same power that raised Jesus lives
in me—I am unshakable.

I am resilient, restored, and ready for
all God has called me to.

I am resilient in the face of adversity.

I trust that challenges will not define me but
will shape me into a stronger person.

With each trial I overcome, my spirit is uplifted,
and I am empowered to inspire others.

I embrace my journey with courage, knowing that I can
do all things through Christ who strengthens me.

Release Prayer:

Dear God, I thank You for being my anchor
during turbulent times.

I come to You with a heart burdened by struggles and
trials, and I ask for Your strength to endure.

Help me see my challenges as opportunities
for growth and transformation.

Please grant me the courage to face each obstacle with grace and the wisdom to learn from my experiences.

May I always remember that my resilience comes from You, and may I be a beacon of hope and strength for others. Amen.

Day Eleven

The Art of Letting Go and Letting God Lead Your Life

Transitioning from resilience to release, we find ourselves at a crossroads. The place where surrender becomes the very act of strength. True resilience is not only found in weathering storms but also in knowing when to release our burdens and trust the One who holds our future. Letting go is not forgetting nor abandoning hope; instead, it is an act of faith that opens our hands to receive God's guidance and grace.

Surrender is the gateway to peace when I reflect on a time I tried to control everything in my life whew, let me tell you, I'm the person who has a planner and I plan on what the year going to be and what trips we're taking for the year, to monthly goals, 3 month goals to yearly goals that I want to accomplish. I mean, your girl is detailed and organized, but I will admit that's how I keep it together because my life is busy, and everybody needs something.

If you're married or have kids, you can relate. Mom/Wife keeps the household together. Well, let's just say two years ago I planned and had everything in order till I didn't when life hit, and I was no longer in control. My plans failed, and I had to allow someone else to take the lead and steer my life.

As we embrace this new day, we are invited to relinquish control and invite God to lead our lives. This journey calls us to trust that His wisdom far exceeds our understanding and that, when we let go, we allow space for healing, transformation, and profound peace. A breakthrough moment is when I said my life isn't my own, lord I need you to help me I realized that a schedule didn't matter, and all the planning and time I put in didn't matter anymore. In that moment, I released my control over every area of my life.

Letting go can often feel like a daunting challenge. We cling to memories, people, and experiences and fearing that release means losing a part of ourselves. Yet, letting go is a vital step toward healing and purposeful growth. It frees us from the chains of the past and prepares our hearts for the new blessings God has in store. Through faith, reflection, and acceptance, we learn that surrender is not weakness, but the courageous act of placing our lives fully in God's hands.

I will be honest; a lot has changed in my life since I fully put my trust in God. I now wake up and pray, and I ask God to order my steps as I go throughout my day, and allow me to be a blessing to someone. Throughout my daily im spending time with him through listening to the word of god on YouTube or taking the time to open up my bible. My life is different, and daily I seek to know him more and more.

Here are a few steps of encouragement that you can use as a guide. It doesn't have to be all deep, but authentic, and take steps.

Embrace Change:

Life's seasons are always shifting, each with its own meaning and mission. Ecclesiastes 3:1 assures us, "There is a time for everything, and a season for every activity under the heavens." Accepting change as part of God's design allows us to move forward with open hearts and hopeful spirits.

Release Control:

The desire to control every outcome can breed anxiety and unrest. Proverbs 19:21 reminds us, "Many are the plans in a person's heart, but it is the LORD's purpose that prevails." By trusting in God's plan, we surrender our illusions of control and find rest in His sovereignty.

Forgiveness Is Freedom:

Release is impossible without forgiveness—for ourselves and for others. Ephesians 4:32 encourages, "Be kind and compassionate to one another, forgiving each other, just as in Christ God forgave you." Forgiveness liberates us from old wounds and paves the way for renewal and grace.

Let Go of Regret:

Regret can tether us to what cannot be changed. Philippians 3:13-14 inspires, "Forgetting what is behind and straining toward what is ahead, I press on toward the goal." By letting go of regret, we allow ourselves to focus on the present and anticipate the future God has prepared.

Trust in God's Timing:

Surrender means accepting that God's timing is perfect, even when it differs from our own. Waiting is not wasted when it draws us nearer to Him and shapes our hearts for what's next.

Letting go is, in truth, letting God. Every act of surrender is an invitation for Him to take the lead, to transform our scars into testimonies, and to turn our setbacks into stories of victory. When you entrust your journey to God, you discover that you are never letting go into emptiness, but into the loving arms of the One who knows you fully and loves you unconditionally.

May you walk forward with courage, trusting that God will guide each step, heal every wound, and write a story of hope and redemption through your willingness to let go and let God lead your life Letting go isn't easy, but it's an important step toward emotional and spiritual health. As you release what no longer serves you, you create space for new and beautiful things to enter your life. Trust in God's love and guidance, and remember that you're not alone on this journey.

Scripture:

Cast your cares on the LORD, and he will sustain you; he will never let the righteous be shaken." — Psalm 55:22 (NIV)

Reflection/Journal:

What do I need to release today?

Affirmations:

I choose to release what no longer serves my journey.

I honor my past, but do not let it define my future. I am open to new possibilities and trust in God's perfect timing.

With courage, I embrace the art of letting go because I believe in the goodness that lies ahead.

Release Prayer:

Dear Heavenly Father,
I come before You with a heart longing to release the burdens I carry.

Help me let go of my fears, regrets, and attachments that hold me back from experiencing the fullness of life you have for me.

Teach me to embrace change and trust in Your plan. Please give me the strength to forgive and move forward with a lighter spirit.

May I find peace in letting go and joy in the new beginnings that await. Thank you for your guidance and love. In Jesus' name, I pray, Amen

Day Twelve

Community and Support

Healing is not meant to happen alone. As I reflect on a time when I had the support of the community, I'm thankful for different business owners who I supported by purchasing weekly meals for us to eat while I recovered, and my child's teachers who checked on me and were very supportive of my child during my healing process. I'm also very thankful to some awesome women of God who came over to my house, and we watched movies together, and they helped around my house as needed.

I remember telling them I would always value their friendship because I'm the type I don't just let people in my house or in my space. But anytime I needed them, they were there to sit with me at the hospital, asking questions and demanding answers from the doctors. Which tickled me that they were ready to go to battle on my behalf. Get you a support team that will say "Lace up your boots and put on your backpack; it's time to ride!!"

I would also like to share something awesome I learned about a season of isolation vs. connection. A season of isolation serves as a time for personal reflection and to deepen your understanding and relationship with God. God uses those seasons of being alone and isolated to draw us closer to him, to refine and mold us.

Jesus and Moses regularly withdrew to spend time in

solitude and prayer with God. A season of connection is the daily active participation in the body of believers for living out your faith journey. What's exciting is that a season of isolation vs. connection is not to choose which one to do, but to embrace the balance between them.

I have experienced both where it was a long season of being alone and isolated, and in that season, it was painful and full of brokenness. I often describe it as God broke me down to restore me. It was the best time of my life because Growth and development happened, and God was able to strip everything in my life that wasn't giving him Glory. In this season, I was able to identify my purpose. During difficult times, the importance of community and support cannot be overstated. We are not meant to face life alone. From the very beginning, God created us for connection. A strong support system can offer comfort, strength, and hope when we are overwhelmed by our burdens.

Here is how to find or build a healing community by discerning healthy vs. toxic support:

God's design for community in Genesis 2:18, God says, "It is not good for the man to be alone." This highlights our natural need for companionship and support. Being part of a caring community allows us to share our joys and sorrows, finding strength in unified hearts.

Sometimes, all we need is someone to listen to us. James 1:19 encourages us to be "quick to listen, slow to speak. Being there for others fosters connection and offers the comfort they need during tough times. Offering Help to someone, Galatians 6:2 reminds us, "Carry each other's burdens, and in this way, you will fulfill the law of Christ." When we offer our help, we not only lighten someone else's load but also strengthen our community bonds.

The Gift of Sharing Testimonies: Our stories have power. Revelation 12:11 tells us, "They triumphed over him by the blood of the Lamb and by the word of their testimony." Sharing our past struggles can motivate others and remind us that healing is possible.

Matthew 18:20 assures us, "For where two or three gather in my name, there am I with them." Prayer strengthens our community. Praying together can foster an environment of hope, helping us lean on one another in faith.

Building Healthy Connections means surrounding yourself with people who uplift and support you. 1 Thessalonians 5:11 encourages us, "Therefore, encourage one another and build each other up." Seek friendships that reflect God's love and grace.

This one is my favorite one, and I had to learn this too. Accepting Help: It's okay to ask for help. Philippians 2:4 encourages us to "look not only to our interests, but also to the interests of others." Welcome support to build stronger relationships and communities.

Let's learn to Celebrate Together. Community isn't just about offering support during tough times; it's also about rejoicing in victories. Romans 12:15 urges us to "Rejoice with those who rejoice; mourn with those who mourn." Sharing both joyful and sorrowful moments builds stronger bonds.

During difficult times, remember you're not alone. God has put people in your life to walk with you. Value your community and be willing to both receive help and give it in return.

Scripture:

For where two or three gather in my name, there am I with them. Matthew 18:20 (NIV)

Reflection/Journal:

Who is in my healing circle?

Affirmations:

I value community in my life.

I am open to accepting support and dedicating myself to being a source of strength and comfort for others.

I understand I am not alone, and I choose to embrace the love and connection God offers through my relationships.

Together, we can lift each other and grow in faith.

Release Prayer:

Dear God,

Thank you for the gift of the community and the support of those around me.

Help me embrace relationships that uplift and encourage me, while also allowing me to be a source of comfort for others.

Teach me to lean on my brothers and sisters in faith when I am weary and to offer my strength when they are in need.

May our connections reflect Your love and grace. I trust in

Your plan for my life and the people You have placed in it.

Thank you for never allowing me to walk alone. In Jesus' name, I pray, Amen.

Day Thirteen

Healing Through Creativity

At every stage of life, creativity offers a way to heal and find hope. Creating—whether through words, colors, melodies, movement, or other forms of expression—helps us uncover parts of ourselves that may be hidden or hurting. When we bring our inner world into the light through creative actions, we encourage healing and change. Creativity serves as a doorway to renewal.

Creativity isn't just reserved for the gifted or famous; it is a gift from God, woven into every person's fabric. In Genesis 1:27, we learn that we are made in God's image, and because of this, our desire and ability to create reflect the divine nature within us. When we pick up a paintbrush, write a heartfelt poem, or sing a melody from the depths of our soul, we are echoing the heart of the Creator.

A creative outlet that has brought healing to me is dance, especially when I get to dance in His presence. Every time I have the chance to use my body as a form of worship, I feel a deep connection. Every time I wave a flag, it's a prophetic declaration—my movement with the flag is my way of making a statement in the spirit realm, declaring God's truth, power, and authority over every space or situation.

Flags enable you to engage your entire being—body, soul, and spirit—in worship. This can help shift the atmosphere, release a spirit of heaviness, and invite God's presence. It is an intimate, personal act of offering praise to God. As you worship, the Holy Spirit can guide your movements, making it a form of personal prayer and intercession.

As I reflect, I think about how even in pain, I still dedicate myself to the Father. It's been many times I was just leaving the hospital, and I still got up to praise His name. I would basically wrap myself in my bandages, double layer my garments, and grab my flag to go minister. I felt like this is where my peace comes from, and this is where my healing will come through. So, I will always worship Him, no matter how I feel in my body. This was my way of expressing pain through creativity.

The role that creativity in praise dance plays in my purpose today is that it offers a powerful outlet for self-expression, deepens spiritual connection, and inspires a wider community. My creative dance movements reflect my spiritual journey, helping to clarify my purpose for what I do. It also enables others to discover their purpose through dance. I can help others express what's inside of them and connect with what God is calling them to do.

In this, there is spiritual expression and worship: honoring God through praise and worship. Dancers can use their bodies to express the divine and convey the word of God through dance. It reflects the work of the Holy Spirit, as well as expresses joy, victory, and deliverance.
Ministry and outreach are essential in helping build the kingdom of God. We are able to spread the gospel through praise dancing because it allows us to communicate God's message to His people, and it helps to reach the lost. You can also minister to others in various ways.

I believe praise dance can go beyond the church walls and reach the nations because there are people in nursing homes, hospitals, and other places to share the gospel with. I personally enjoy dancing outside the walls. I remember going to nursing homes and dancing, seeing the smiles on their faces as I or my team ministered. It brought them great joy because, honestly, some of them don't get visitors, so seeing someone come by makes them happy.

Also, when I think about going to Children's Levine Hospital to dance during Christmas time, I'm very grateful for that moment. You don't realize how blessed you are until you walk in there and see all the children and families facing daily struggles. It gives you a different perspective on life. So, I challenge you to go deeper in your creation and to use everything God has given you.

A Canvas for the Soul: Engaging in creative activities provides a safe space to process and express emotions that words alone can't always capture. Whether painting, sculpting, crafting, journaling, or any other form of creative expression, we give voice to feelings that may be deeply tangled inside. Each brushstroke, stanza, or note becomes a prayer, a release, and a step toward healing.

Creativity as Communion: Our creative pursuits can act as acts of worship—intimate moments when we invite God into our process. As we create with open hearts, we draw nearer to God, praising Him not only with words but also through the work of our hands. Psalm 150 encourages us to praise God with music and dance; whatever medium we choose, let it be an offering that honors Him.

Encountering God Through the Act of Creation: There is a special presence that often accompanies the creative process. As we lose ourselves in the flow of creating, we discover new facets of God's character and are reminded of His attention to detail, beauty, and order. Creativity keeps us rooted in the present moment, allowing us to experience God's peace and comfort right where we are.

The Healing Power of Story: Sharing our stories, whether through writing, art, or spoken words, is a courageous act that can bring healing to ourselves and to those who listen. Telling our stories breaks isolation and creates connections. Revelation 12:11 reminds us of the power in testimony; as we bear witness to our journeys, we inspire hope and encourage others on their own path to healing.

Freedom in the Creative Process: Creativity releases us from perfectionism and self-judgment. It's not about producing a masterpiece but about giving ourselves permission to play, explore, and express. In this freedom, we often discover joy, resilience, and a deeper sense of identity as beloved children of God.

Let creativity become a source of renewal in your life. Whether you're writing, painting, singing, building, or simply daydreaming, see these moments as opportunities to heal, connect, and remember that you are never alone on your journey. Through creativity, God whispers truth, comfort, and hope, restoring us from the inside out.

Creativity is a powerful outlet for expressing emotions and healing. When we engage in creative activities—such as art, writing, music, or other forms of self-expression—we give ourselves a chance to process feelings that might be too overwhelming to put into words. This devotional day looks at how creativity can be a healing tool and a way to connect with God through our expressions. Here are some practical ways to channel scars into art: Start by expressing yourself.

Engaging in creative activities provides a way to express inner struggles. Whether through painting, writing poetry, or playing an instrument, these outlets offer opportunities to explore emotions and release what we may be holding inside. Colossians 3:23 reminds us, "Whatever you do, work at it with all your heart, as working for the Lord."

Art as a Form of Worship: Art can serve as a deeply personal way to express our connection with God. When we create from a place of vulnerability, we invite God to be part of our creative process. Psalm 150:1 encourages us to praise the Lord through music and dance. Let your creativity become a form of praise that reflects your heart's most genuine desires and struggles.

Discovering God in the Process: Creativity encourages presence and mindfulness, creating a space where we can meet God. During moments of creation, we can reflect on His beauty and the details of His creation. Genesis 1:27 tells us that we are made in God's image, meaning our creativity mirrors His divine nature.

Healing Through Storytelling: Sharing our stories, whether through writing or speaking, can be a healing and therapeutic experience. Our stories can connect with and inspire others. Revelation 12:11 says, "They triumphed over him by the blood of the Lamb and by the word of their testimony." Your story is important and can motivate others on their journey to healing.

Freedom in Creation: In creative expression, there are no right or wrong answers, allowing us to shed the weight of expectations. This freedom can be liberating and healing. Isaiah 61:3 speaks of God providing "a garment of praise instead of a spirit of despair." Embrace creativity to turn your pain into beauty.

Community and Collaboration: Participating in creative activities with others fosters connection and support. God designed us for community and teamwork. Ecclesiastes 4:12 reminds us that a cord of three strands is not easily broken. Working together allows healing to flow as we share our gifts.

Journaling as a Reflection Tool: Keeping a journal can help process emotions, thoughts, and prayers. It provides a safe space for introspection and exploration. Psalm 77:12 states, "I will consider all your work and meditate on all your mighty deeds." Writing allows us to reflect on how God has moved in our lives, fostering healing and gratitude.

Scripture:

"He has filled them with skill to do all kinds of work."
Exodus 35:35

"I praise you because I am fearfully and wonderfully made; your works are wonderful; I know that full well." Psalm 139:14 (NIV)

Reflection/Journal:

How can I use creativity to handle pain?

How can creativity heal me?

What creative outlets resonate with me?

Affirmations:

I have come to value the healing power of creativity in my life.

I realize that my unique gifts and expressions are part of God's divine plan.

As I create, I release my worries and fears, allowing joy and peace to flow through me.

I trust that through my creativity, I am refreshed and renewed, and I open myself to the transformative energy that surrounds me.

Release Prayer:

Dear God,

I come before You, seeking healing through my creativity.

Thank you for the gift of expression and the unique ways I can reflect your beauty.

Help me release any fear of judgment or criticism and embrace the freedom that comes with creating.

Guide my hands and heart as I create, allowing each stroke of a brush, word on a page, or note played to be an offering of praise to You.

May my creativity become a pathway to healing, connecting me with You and others on a deeper level. I trust that in my vulnerability, I can find strength, purpose, and renewal.

Thank you for being my constant companion on this journey. In Jesus' name, I pray, Amen.

Embrace creativity as a crucial part of your healing journey, using it to connect more deeply with God while finding freedom and renewal through your expressive pursuits.

Day Fourteen

Honoring Mental Health Through Creativity and Faith

Let's discuss a very tough topic that most people don't like to talk about: mental health. I will say it...your mental health matters, and I strongly believe that faith and creativity can nurture it. I think it's very important to balance faith and health during challenging times. Here's why: when you're dealing with a diagnosis or certain events in your life, your mental state becomes extremely important. God wants us to have a sound mind.

I must be honest because there were many times during my journey when my mental health was challenged, and I felt so overwhelmed. You might be thinking, well, ain't you saved? So why do you feel like that? Well, I must admit I got weak and weary. The more I went to the doctor, the more I heard there's no cure, and we need to do another surgery, and now you have this going on, and you might not have any more kids, but you could get a surrogate.

Whew, that's a lot to process. But in that moment, I felt overwhelmed, and that's when that sound mind came into play. I had to bounce back and speak life, no doubt, and no unbelief. This is how faith comes into play.

Faith works by hearing the word of God and renewing your mind. You must activate your faith in every season of your life. Good or bad, you must lean on what you believe, and that's what

I did. I trust God, and it didn't matter what the doctors' reports said; I believe God. Guess what, I still to this day have some health problems I'm dealing with, but I still believe the word of God, and I believe that I'm going to live to see it happen in my life. A miracle shall be performed in Jesus' name.

That's how faith and creativity become your lifeline because you're seeking God daily while walking in purpose or the plan He has for your life. I suggest taking steps daily to help with your mental health, faith, therapy, and creativity can coexist, and you can start by journaling. That's where I started; I just bought a journal, and I started to write what was on the tablet of my heart. It was like me and God were having a conversation, and in my journal, I would just let it out and let it flow.

Keeping a journal is more than just recording daily events; it becomes a beautiful space where emotions, thoughts, and prayers come together. Through writing, we create a refuge for self-reflection and gentle exploration, drawing inspiration from Psalm 77:12: "I will consider all your work and meditate on all your mighty deeds." As we document moments of God's intervention in our lives, journaling turns into an act of healing and gratitude, revealing patterns of grace and resilience.

As you engage in journaling or other creative pursuits, remember that honoring your mental health is a journey marked by intention and compassion. Each word you write, image you create, or melody you compose can become an act of surrender and a gentle release of what burdens you and an invitation to healing. Let creativity be a form of prayer, a safe space where your innermost struggles, hopes, and joys can surface without fear of judgment.

Through consistent reflective practice, you may notice themes of God's faithfulness woven through even the darkest chapters. Creativity and faith come together to illuminate meaning in your experiences, helping you recognize moments of growth and signs of grace you might otherwise overlook. Trust that God delights in your honest offerings, no matter how incomplete or imperfect they seem.

In this beautiful dance of creativity and faith, mental wellness becomes not just a goal, but a way of being—one shaped by gratitude, authenticity, and openness to God's loving presence. As you honor your mental health, let self-compassion and hope lead your steps, understanding that healing happens gradually, like a masterpiece created over time.

Scripture:

"Do not be anxious about anything."

Philippians 4:6

"Beloved, I pray you prosper in health."

3 John 1:2

Reflection/Journal:

How do faith and creativity support my mental health?

Affirmation:

I have a sound mind

Release Prayer:

Dear Heavenly Father,

I come before You with a heart seeking healing. Help me recognize the importance of my mental health and release any burdens weighing heavily on my spirit.

Please grant me the courage to seek the support I deserve

and surround myself with positive influences.

As I begin this journey toward healing, fill me with Your love and guidance.

Bless me with peace and joy and help me stay mindful of the hope and future You have prepared for me. In Jesus' name, I pray, Amen.

Day Fifteen

*Embracing Change: Stepping Forward
with Courage and Grace*

Change is part of the healing journey. Change comes into our lives not as an intruder, but as a catalyst; an invitation to step forward, to evolve, and to shape our stories intentionally. Too often, we view change with suspicion or dread, clinging to what is familiar. But true transformation requires that we meet change where it stands: with open hands, a courageous heart, and unwavering faith.

A season when I resisted change was when I realized God was calling me higher. I knew there was a purpose for me on the earth; I just didn't know what it was. I will be honest, I ignored the signs and ran for a good while, but then it was as if things in my life started to shift and the places I used to go, I didn't desire to go anymore. I began to want to be home more and in my own space. Or with people I used to hang out with, I started to prefer being alone. And I knew that was strange because I love people and enjoy spending time with them. But that's when the separation came, and the elevation began.

It was necessary because, believe it or not, during this change, He was working on me and the things that needed to be done in my life. If I had kept going down the same path, I wouldn't be able to say I've been changed. It's just like the song Tamela Mann sings,"a wonderful change has come over me.'

This is your moment to stand tall.

When life's seasons shift and when routines unravel, relationships change, or unexpected trials arise, know that you are not powerless. Inside you lies a deep well of resilience and creative potential. Embracing change means daring to trust that wellspring, believing in your ability to face the unknown with strength and wisdom from within and from God above.

I remember starting a new chapter in my life by changing my career. I always worked with children, but it was always in a daycare setting. Sometimes I babysat for date nights and other occasions. One day, I decided I was going to pursue a career as a nanny. I had heard a few coworkers discuss the benefits of being a nanny and a classroom teacher. So, I took the step and inquired about it. I can honestly say it's the best decision I've ever made. I also admit that it's only by the grace of God that I've been able to get through this change in my life.

Standing Firm in Uncertainty

Change is rarely comfortable, but it always offers a chance for growth. When you face new situations, remember that feeling uncomfortable is not a sign of failure; it shows you're pushing beyond old limits. Use every uneasy moment as a reminder of your worth and your ability to adapt. You are defined not by what you lose, but by what you choose to become.

Scripture:

"For I am about to do something new. See, I have already begun! Do you not see it? I will make a pathway through the wilderness. I will create rivers in the dry wasteland." Isaiah 43:19(NLT)

"For everything there is a season, a time for every activity under heaven."

Ecclesiastes 3:1(NLT)

Reflection/Journal:

What changes am I resisting that maybe for my good?

How can I embrace them with courage?

Affirmation:

Today, I declare that I am anchored in hope, embracing the new paths set before me with courage and trust.

I believe that God is guiding my steps, even when the journey feels uncertain.

I let go of fear and open my heart to transformation, knowing that every change is an opportunity for growth.

I am resilient, creative, and filled with divine strength. God's love surrounds me, and His promises sustain me.

I step into this day with faith, expecting miracles and welcoming the blessings that are unfolding in my life. Amen.

Release Prayer:

Gracious God,

Today, I surrender every uncertainty, anxious thought, and burden that weighs upon my heart.

I release my need for control and invite Your peace to fill the spaces where worry once lived.

May Your Spirit calm my restless mind and gentle my steps as I walk into new seasons.

I trust that You are already at work in every detail of my life, preparing pathways of provision and hope.

Let each change I face become an opportunity to witness Your faithfulness.

When fear whispers, remind me of Your promises; when I feel alone, surround me with Your presence.

Grant me the courage to step forward with confidence, knowing that Your wisdom guides me, your love sustains me, and Your grace is sufficient for each new day.

I open my hands and heart to receive all You have prepare for renewal, restoration, and unexpected blessings.

May my life be a testimony of faith that shines in uncertainty, and may I walk boldly into the future, upheld by Your unfailing strength.

In Jesus' name, Amen.

Day Sixteen

The Power of Faith's Impact

Faith changes how we see scars. Faith and spirituality greatly shape the healing journey, guiding us through tough times. When we trust in faith, we find a strong source of strength and resilience. This belief not only offers comfort but also gives us a sense of purpose and meaning during our struggles.

Faith has positively transformed my life because, without it, I don't know how I would have endured the tough times or even gotten through the dark moments. My testimony is that God has already healed me; that's me saying I believe in faith, and that alone will change my outcome when doctors say there is no cure. God is the cure, and He can heal all diseases.

In times of despair, faith acts as a refuge, reassuring us that we are not alone; there's a higher power walking beside us. This sense of companionship can lessen the weight of loneliness and fear, allowing us to face challenges head-on. Believing in a greater plan helps us see our experiences not just as obstacles, but as opportunities for growth and change. While reflecting on moments when my health was affected and everything seemed overwhelming, faith gave me hope to win against all odds.

Spirituality also encourages us to look beyond ourselves. It invites reflection on our place in the world, fostering a sense of connection with others and the divine. This interconnectedness can be healing and sharing our burdens with a faith community can offer support and upliftment, creating a strong network of love and encouragement.

Additionally, faith encourages hope. During tough times, holding onto hope can spark a sense of inner strength. It pushes us to take steps toward healing, whether that's by seeking professional help, engaging in creative activities, or simply putting self-care first. The belief that healing is possible motivates us to keep going, even when the path isn't clear.

Ultimately, faith and spirituality can be powerful forces that transform our lives. They guide the healing process by helping us embrace our vulnerabilities while giving us the strength to overcome them. Through prayer, meditation, and the support of our faith communities, we can navigate our healing journeys with grace and find peace amid struggles. In this way, faith becomes more than just a belief; it becomes a strong ally in our pursuit of wholeness and renewal.

Scripture:

"Now faith is confidence in what we hope for and assurance about what we do not see." — Hebrews 11:1 (NIV)

Faith as small as a mustard seed. Matthew 17:20

Reflection/Journal:

"Where has faith impacted my story most?"

Daily Faith Declarations:

I have come to embrace the transformative power of faith in my life.

I believe that my beliefs shape my reality, and with faith,
I can overcome challenges and achieve my dreams.

I am confident that, as I act on my faith, I will see miracles
and doors opening in ways I never imagined.

My faith energizes my hope, and I am grateful
for the endless possibilities it offers.

Release Prayer:

Dear God,

I come before You, acknowledging the
profound impact of faith in my life.

Thank you for instilling in me a belief that moves
mountains and ignites hope in the darkest of times.

Help me to release any doubts that may hinder my journey
and to trust in Your divine plan for me entirely.

May my faith grow stronger with each challenge I face,
and may it inspire others to seek You as well.

I ask for your guidance as I navigate my path, and I trust that
with you, all things are possible. In Jesus' name, I pray, Amen.

Embrace faith as a guiding force in your life, allowing
it to illuminate your path and inspire you to trust
God's promises as you move forward.

Day Seventeen

Defining My Worth

Worth is not determined by scars but by our identity in God. In a world that often tries to gauge our value through external achievements, validation, and comparison, it's crucial to focus inward. The journey of self-love and self-acceptance is more than just a popular concept; it's a powerful and transformative way to recognize our true worth as individuals. Understanding and embracing who we are deep inside can lead to personal growth and help build more authentic, meaningful relationships with others.

I remember a time in my life when I felt unworthy to worship God or even serve Him because of my scars. See, society and the stares of people can put you in a box and silence your voice. Back then, I believed I needed to be completely cleaned up before I could give God my all. I had done so much in my life, and whew, if you knew my story, you wouldn't want to see me praising God. But we serve a God who wants us to come as we are, even in our mess.

He seeks us out right where we are. That's how God found me...right in my mess, not perfect, not all together, but He met me at that moment, and that's when I started discovering my true worth. I had to remember these things to separate self-worth from performance, pain, or approval. I began by recognizing my unique value.

Before we can cultivate self-love, we must first acknowledge the unique qualities that define us. In Psalms 139:14, it states, "I praise You because I am fearfully and wonderfully made." This truth shows that each of us is intentionally created, with one-of-a-kind gifts, strengths, and experiences that add to our value. Start by taking a moment to reflect on what you love about yourself. Maybe it's your empathy, creativity, resilience, or sense of humor. Recognizing these traits is the starting point for embracing your self-worth.

Then you confront negative self-talk. Often, our inner dialogue can become our greatest adversary. Negative self-talk creates an internal narrative that can diminish our self-esteem. Romans 12:2 encourages us not to conform to the patterns of this world but to be transformed by the renewing of our minds. When you catch yourself in a cycle of self-doubt or criticism, challenge those thoughts. Replace them with affirmations that reinforce your worth. Remind yourself that you deserve love and respect, just as you are. Embrace imperfection.

In a society that often promotes perfectionism, it's important to accept our flaws and imperfections. Perfection is an illusion that can cause feelings of inadequacy. Recognizing that we are all a "work in progress" helps us accept ourselves, both our strengths and weaknesses. As Paul writes in 2 Corinthians 12:9, "My grace is sufficient for you, for my power is made perfect in weakness." Embracing imperfection not only shows authenticity but also encourages personal growth and self-compassion.

Establish healthy boundaries. Self-love involves respecting yourself enough to set boundaries. Knowing when to say no and prioritizing your well-being are essential parts of self-acceptance. Galatians 6:5 encourages us to "carry each other's burdens," but it's just as important not to take on the weight of others at the expense of our mental and emotional health. Surround yourself with people who uplift and support you, while also understanding that it's okay to step back from relationships that drain your energy.

Prioritize self-care. Self-love is more than just a mindset; it shows how we care for ourselves. Spend time nurturing your physical, emotional, and spiritual health. This might mean pursuing a hobby that brings you happiness, taking long walks in nature, or practicing your spirituality through prayer and meditation. 1 Corinthians 6:19 reminds us that our bodies are temples of the Holy Spirit; taking care of ourselves is a way of honoring the life we've been given.

Celebrate Your Achievements: Take time to recognize even the small victories in your life. Whether it's finishing a task, overcoming a challenge, or simply making it through a tough day, acknowledging these moments builds a sense of achievement and boosts your self-worth. As Paul states in Philippians 4:4, "Rejoice in the Lord always." Developing an attitude of gratitude can change our perspective on our journey and improve our self-acceptance.

Surround Yourself with Positivity. The people we surround ourselves with can greatly influence how we see ourselves. Build relationships that uplift and motivate you. Find individuals who support your growth and celebrate your progress. As Proverbs 27:17 states, "As iron sharpens iron, so one person sharpens another." Being around positive people will help boost your self-worth and acceptance.

My view of myself back then was that I wasn't good enough to be loved by friends, family, or partners. I was just existing and going through the motions of life with no concern because I couldn't care less about your feelings. I saw my worth from a different perspective, but now that I know my value and who I am, I see a Queen. My standards are higher now, and I no longer settle for the bare minimum from anyone. I know people might think I'm cocky or bougie, but I'm not; it's the God-confidence I walk in daily. I walk with my head high and step boldly into any door I want to walk through, expecting great things.

In conclusion, defining our worth through self-love and acceptance is a lifelong journey. It requires intentional practice, patience, and a commitment to nurturing ourselves. By recognizing our unique value, challenging negative thoughts, embracing imperfections, setting boundaries, investing in self-care, celebrating achievements, and surrounding ourselves with positivity, we can start to understand and appreciate our true worth. Remember, you are wonderfully made, deserving of love and respect, not just from others but from yourself. As you begin this path of self-discovery, trust that you are exactly who you're meant to be. Embrace your journey with compassion and let your light shine brightly.

Scripture:

You are worth more than many sparrows.

Luke 12:6-7

Reflection/Journal:

What lies have I believed about my worth?

How do I define my worth?

Affirmations:

I am created in the image of God, and my worth is innate and priceless.

I choose to embrace my unique qualities and talents, knowing that I have a purpose and a place in this world.

I release the need for external validation and confidently recognize that my value comes from within.

I am deserving of love, respect, and happiness, and I celebrate who I am becoming.

Release Prayer:

Dear God,

I come before You, seeking clarity and confirmation of my worth. Thank you for creating me in Your image and for the unique qualities You have given me.

Help me recognize and appreciate the gifts I have and let go of any doubts or negative thoughts that lessen my self-esteem.

Guide me to embrace my identity as Your beloved creation and strengthen me to resist comparing myself to others.

May I find peace in knowing I am enough just as I am. Surround me with Your unconditional love as I move toward self-acceptance and confidence.

In Jesus' name, I pray, Amen.

Embrace your worth every day, remembering that it is shaped by God's love and the unique purpose He has for your life.

Day Eighteen

Facing Fears Head-On

Courage is walking toward what once paralyzed you. As I reflect on the fear of being an entrepreneur and pursuing multiple streams of income, I can admit that fear controlled my decision to stay stuck and comfortable. See, God had given me different visions of things, and I would simply write them down; whatever I saw in the dream, I would put on paper and leave it. I did that for several years, just clocking in at my job, but while working, all we talked about was ownership and wanting to start this business and that business. Or I would push them to think bigger than where they were at that time.

Then came the moment I chose to confront my fear of going after what I wanted, and even though I haven't opened every business I planned, I strive daily to work toward it. Every day, I hear God saying, "Use everything I put in your hands." My hands are created to do many things, which is why I pursue multiple streams of income. Victory looks good on the other side, when you can be a blessing to others and not struggle day to day. I find joy in knowing that God is going to make me the blesser who can help others.

Fear is a universal emotion that can hold us back from pursuing our dreams and fully engaging with life. However, facing our fears head-on is essential for growth and can boost self-confidence and resilience.

So, let's explore practical ways to confront and overcome

fears, empowering us to move forward with courage and determination. Fear often grows in silence but diminishes when faced. Here are some steps to guide you toward confronting your fears:

Identify Your Fears: The first step in overcoming fear is recognizing what we are afraid of. Take time to reflect on your fears. Consider whether they are related to failure, rejection, loss, or the unknown. Writing them down can help clarify their nature and the impact they have on your life. Understanding your fears is essential for tackling them head-on.

Challenge Your Thoughts: Often, our fears are caused by negative or irrational thoughts. Question these thoughts by asking yourself: "Is this fear-based reality or?" or "What evidence supports or contradicts this fear?" Replacing negative thoughts with more balanced and positive ones can help shift your perspective and reduce anxiety.

Take Small Steps: Facing fears can feel overwhelming, but breaking them down into smaller, manageable steps makes the process less intimidating. Every step you take, no matter how small, is a victory. For example, if you fear public speaking, start by practicing in front of a mirror, then speak in front of a friend, and gradually move up to larger audiences.

Visualize Success: Visualization is a powerful tool for overcoming fear. Spend time imagining yourself succeeding despite your fear. Visualize the details: how you feel, what you see, and how others react. This mental practice can boost confidence and promote a positive mindset, making it easier to face fear when it occurs.

Seek Support: You don't have to confront your fears alone.

Sharing them with trusted friends, family, or a support group can lessen the burden and boost your confidence. Others might offer new perspectives or strategies you haven't thought of, and knowing you're supported can strengthen your resolve.

Practice mindfulness and relaxation techniques: Fear often triggers a stress response in our bodies. Engaging in mindfulness, deep breathing, or relaxation exercises can help anchor you in the present and calm your nerves. Methods like meditation, yoga, or even taking a walk in nature can help lessen fear and anxiety, making it easier to confront what you're afraid of.

Reframe the Fear of Failure:

Fear of failure can hold us back from taking risks. However, it's crucial to change how we see failure. Instead of viewing it as a setback, think of it as a chance to learn. Every failure offers valuable lessons that help us grow and improve. Adopting this mindset can lessen the hold of fear.

Set Practical Goals: Defining clear and achievable goals related to your fears can serve as a guide for progress. Instead of trying to conquer your fear all at once, concentrate on specific, realistic objectives that promote steady improvement. Celebrate each milestone to stay motivated.

Expose Yourself to Your Fears: Gradual exposure is a proven way to conquer fear. It involves intentionally facing situations that cause anxiety in a controlled setting. Begin with less intimidating scenarios and gradually move on to more challenging ones, helping you become less sensitive to fear over time.

Reflect on Your Progress: Make time regularly to think about how far you've come. Notice every step you've taken toward facing your fears, no matter how small. Keeping a journal can help you record your experiences, thoughts, and feelings as you confront your fears and monitor your progress.

Scriptures:

For I am not giving you a spirit of fear, but of power, love, and self-discipline. 2 Timothy 1:7 (NIV)

When I am afraid, I put my trust in you. Psalm 56:3 (NIV)

So do not fear, for I am with you; do not be dismayed, for I am your God. I will strengthen you and help you; I will uphold you with my righteous right hand." — Isaiah 41:10 (NIV)

These scriptures remind us of God's presence and strength, encouraging us to face our fears with confidence and courage. That support carried me through. I am worthy of hope, connection, and joy. Even when the future feels uncertain, I trust in my ability to heal, to dream, and to start anew. My story is unfolding, and I accept it with gratitude and grace.

Reflection/Journal:

What fears hold me back?

How can I face them bravely?

The Lord is my light and salvation; whom shall, I fear? The Lord is the stronghold of my life, whom shall I be afraid? Psalm 27:1 (NIV)

Affirmations:

I have the strength and courage to face my fears. Each day, I choose to take small steps toward overcoming the things that hold me back. I trust in my ability to learn and grow from every challenge I encounter.

Release Prayer:

Dear God,

As I face my fears, I ask for your strength and guidance.

Help me see my fears as chances for growth and learning, not as barriers to happiness.

Please give me the courage to take bold steps to overcome them and the wisdom to learn from my experiences.

Thank you for being with me on this journey, and for reminding me that with you, I am never alone. In Jesus' name, I pray, Amen.

Day Nineteen

Reframing Scars and Embracing the Healing Journey

How you see scars influences how you live with them. Never be ashamed of a scar; remember, a scar that once caused shame can turn into a source of strength. This happens when you change your perspective from viewing your scar as a flaw to seeing it as a symbol of resilience. A scar that once made me feel shame but now gives me strength is the scar of past mistakes. These scars cause me to remember the times I felt regret or guilt over poor choices I made in my life. Just think about it for a moment: when you made a wrong decision and replayed it in your mind repeatedly. You can find strength by learning from those experiences and using wisdom to make better choices in the future. You need to see your scar in a new light and forgive yourself for past mistakes so you won't fall into the same pitfalls.

Facing fears is often one of life's most significant challenges, but with each brave step, new opportunities arise. By employing practical strategies and embracing the process, fear can be transformed into empowerment, leading to a more fulfilling and joyful life.

Reframing the Narrative About Scars and Trauma

Life's challenges often leave scars—both visible and invisible. These marks may serve as reminders of past trauma or suffering, but by changing how we see them, we can transform our perspective. Instead of letting scars define us, we can view them as symbols of survival, resilience, and growth. My testimony of me reframing my perspective is yes I was young and pregnant and unmarried I wouldn't let shame or grief define me I chose use this scar as a reminder to share my story to encourage other young people not to fall for the hype of wanting the fast life and settling for relationships that degrade you.

Acknowledge Your Scars

Healing starts with identifying our scars. Ignoring or hiding pain allows it to worsen, but recognizing physical injuries, emotional wounds, or deep traumas is crucial. Recognition not only fosters healing but also deepens our understanding of how these experiences have shaped us.

Shift from Victimhood to Empowerment

Although it is easy to adopt a victim mindset after trauma, this attitude can lead to feeling helpless. By changing perspective, it becomes clear that we are not defined by what has happened to us. Honoring pain while focusing on the strength gained and resilience built empowers us to find purpose in our scars and to create a narrative rooted in strength.

Embrace the Lessons Learned

Each scar teaches a lesson. Reflecting on experiences and the wisdom gained shows how challenges lead to growth. Seeing scars as chances to learn encourages gratitude. Scars can create meaningful connections, allowing us to offer support based on real empathy and understanding.

Redefining Beauty and Wholeness

In a world that often equates beauty with perfection, it is crucial to redefine what it means to be whole. Scars tell stories of survival and courage, adding depth to a person's character. By choosing to wear scars as badges of honor rather than hiding them, authenticity is embraced, and beauty is found in what makes us unique.

Sharing Your Story

Talking openly about scars can be a powerful step toward healing. Sharing stories builds connections with others who face similar struggles. Vulnerability fosters empathy, encourages understanding, and creates a safe space for others to share their challenges. Stories can inspire hope and show the resilience of the human spirit.

Engage in Creative Expression

Creative activities like art or writing provide powerful ways to process trauma and reshape personal stories. Exploring feelings through creative outlets respects the scars and shows the depth of the journey, whether through painting, journaling, or music.

Seek Support and Community

A supportive community can significantly improve the healing process. Connecting with friends, family, or support groups that understand these barriers helps change one's perspective. Sharing fears, experiences, and successes fosters a sense of belonging and promotes collective encouragement.

Practice Self-Compassion

Reframing the story about scars and trauma requires self-compassion. It's important to be gentle with yourself during the healing process, recognizing that pain and difficulty are part of it. Treating yourself with kindness encourages a positive change in your inner conversation.

Conclusion: Embrace Your Journey

By redefining the narrative around scars and trauma, it becomes possible to fully embrace the journey. Through acknowledgment, empowerment, and connection, scars change from reminders of pain into symbols of resilience and hope. Scars are not just remnants of suffering; they are vital parts of personal stories and growth. Embracing this journey lights a path to strength, courage, and transformation, inspiring others along the way.

Scripture:

All things work together for good.

Romans 8:28

Reflection/Journal:

How can I see scars as strengths?

How has healing shaped me?

Affirmations:

"I embrace my journey and the beauty of my scars"

Release Prayer:

Gracious God, I come before You are seeking renewal for my spirit and clarity for my mind.

Help me to see my life and scars through Your eyes, recognizing the strength and beauty that grow from every challenge.

Restore my hope and refresh my heart, so I may embrace each new day with gratitude and courage.

Shift my perspective, Lord, that I may find purpose in my journey, wisdom in my struggles, and joy in every step forward.

Guide me to trust in Your promises and walk boldly into the future You have prepared for me. Amen.

Day Twenty

The Power of Hope

Hope is the anchor that keeps us steady. Hope isn't the absence of hardship but the steady belief that tomorrow offers the chance of renewal. It quietly rests in the heart, brightening even the darkest corners and inspiring the courage needed to persevere. Sometimes, hope may flicker and be delicate and uncertain. But even the smallest spark can light the way through challenges. By nurturing hope, individuals discover the strength to dream beyond their current pain and envision brighter days despite lingering shadows.

A time when hope was the only thing keeping me moving forward was when I held onto the hope that I would recover from it all. Daily, I endure challenges and setbacks, but victory is on the other side. I celebrate every small victory, focusing on my family's needs, myself and my little girl, who needs her mom to be healed and whole. I'm reminded of the story of Job, which is a powerful example of perseverance and hope in the face of suffering. Job lost his children, wealth, and his health was tested, but despite his trials, Job remained faithful to God. That teaches us that hope can be maintained even during the hardest seasons or darkest moments of your life.

In moments of despair, hope acts as a gentle companion, reminding us that every chapter of life, no matter how daunting, remains unfinished. It encourages us to seek new possibilities, dare to believe in healing, and trust in the gradual process of transformation. Rooted in hope, resilience grows, reminding us that every scar and hardship can become a source of light for ourselves and those who follow our path.

Scripture:

For I know the plans I have for you," declares the Lord, "plans to prosper you and not to harm you, plans to give you hope and a future. Jeremiah 29:11 (NIV)

"Be joyful in hope, patient in affliction." Romans 12:12

Reflection/Journal:

What gives me hope?

How can I cultivate more hope daily?

Affirmations:

I embrace hope as a guiding light in my life.

Even in times of despair and challenge, I choose to believe in the possibility of brighter days ahead.

I am capable of overcoming obstacles and transforming hardships into growth.

Hope fills my heart and inspires my actions

Release Prayer:

Dear God,

In moments of despair, I seek your light to guide me through the darkness.

Please help me to see that hope is alive within me, nurturing my spirit and reminding me of the possibilities ahead.

Please grant me the strength to remain resilient in the face of challenges and the faith to trust in your plan for my life.

Thank you for your unwavering presence
during times of uncertainty.

With you, I find hope anew. In Jesus' name, I pray, Amen.

Day Twenty-One

The Journey of Motherhood

Motherhood is both refining and redemptive. It is a journey characterized by profound transformation, vulnerability, and boundless love. It involves learning, where each day presents challenges and unexpected moments of joy. Through sleepless nights and small victories, mothers discover a resilience they never knew they had. The journey is not about perfection but about the willingness to show up...again and again for those they cherish.

Today let's honor the complexities of motherhood: the delicate balancing act between caring for others and oneself, the bittersweet letting go that comes with children's growth, and the quiet pride that swells when witnessing their milestones. That alone engages our ability and stories of giving, forgiving, and growing alongside our children, recognizing the lessons of motherhood, which often ariss from our mistakes as much as from our successes.

Ultimately, the journey of motherhood is not just about raising children but about transforming oneself. Through love, sacrifice, and hope, mothers shape future generations while discovering deeper aspects of their strength and capacity for compassion.

After being rushed to the hospital because I felt like I was experiencing contractions, I arrived and found out I was already having contractions and was dilated 8 cm. The doctor said that when we reach 10 cm, we would go ahead and deliver the baby.

I was overwhelmed with intense emotions because it wasn't supposed to be the time for me to have my baby, even though her due date was in October.

I began to panic and worry because I had been through this before with my first child, and I needed this delivery to go smoothly. However, the doctors explained the plan and how we would proceed. I delivered my daughter naturally, without epidural or medication. She weighed 2 pounds 14 ounces. They told me that since she came two months early and was considered a preemie, she would be sent to the NICU.

The thought of being in this room while she was taken elsewhere in the hospital upset me, so I started asking all kinds of questions, even neglecting my own health. I wanted to hold my baby right then, but I also wanted them to check her and ensure she was okay. The nurse informed me that after she arrived in the NICU and they ran tests and got her settled, they would call me to come see her.

When that time came, we went over there, and the nurses explained the next steps. I'll admit, the NICU experience isn't easy because you have to wait patiently until they let you hold your baby. My child had to go through a process where she was in an incubator that helped her get everything she would have needed if she was still in my womb. I remember seeing tubes connected to her arms and head.

A significant victory was that she was breathing on her own when she was born; she just needed to gain weight. Her skin tone was developing, and my baby also had a small brain bleed that eventually stopped. I remember it clearly, she stayed in the hospital for two months. I was there every day, praying, singing gospel songs in her ear, and when it was time for skin-to-skin contact or feeding, I covered her from head to toe.

The end of that journey was a celebration; we got to take her home, and our miracle baby had made it through. I recall doctors telling me she might be delayed or face difficulties because of the brain hemorrhage, but she beat the odds. She wasn't delayed in her development; in fact, she met all her milestones on time.

Reflections on Parenting

Parenting is a deep journey filled with moments of happiness, love, and growth, along with challenges that test our strength and determination. As a mother, I've learned that each experience, whether successful or difficult shapes not only my child but also my identity as a parent. From the early days of sleepless nights and countless diaper changes to the bittersweet milestones of watching my child take her first steps, every moment has taught me invaluable lessons about patience, sacrifice, and the power of unconditional love.

As they grow, their unique personalities unfold, and I learn to embrace their individuality, supporting their dreams while recognizing that it's okay for them to stumble and learn from their mistakes. Nurturing a child is also a chance for self-discovery. It pushes me to think about my values and beliefs, helping me become a better person for their benefit. My child reflects me, showing both my strengths and weaknesses, which encourages me to grow with them.

I must admit that balancing motherhood with the physical and emotional scars of a challenging past can sometimes be a trigger for some, but it is necessary for growth and the journey ahead. It's a complex journey of growth, resilience, and complete healing needed for you to show your children that you overcame what once tried to stop you. For many women, motherhood forces us to confront past traumas and hurts, pushing us to process and dig deep into those scars so we can be transformed.

While confronting these wounds, you may find it difficult to face and process them, and you might see that the wounds are ugly with all that has settled in over the years. The love for a child can serve as a catalyst to break cycles of pain.Through these trials and triumphs, I have learned that love is not only about giving but also about being present, listening, nurturing, and celebrating the small victories along the way. As a mother, I value the shared moments, the laughter, and even the tears, knowing they all add to the beautiful story of our family.

My child has taught me many valuable lessons in patience, acceptance, selflessness, and unconditional love. The importance of being present in your child's life. The resilience of kindness and gratitude is about being grateful for what you do have. Motherhood is not about perfection but presence. I want to encourage you to release the guilt of having it all together and embrace grace.

Scripture:

"Children are a heritage from the Lord, offspring a reward from him." — Psalm 127:3 NIV.

Reflection/Journal:

"What has motherhood taught me about healing?"

Affirmations:

As a mother, I embrace the journey of parenting with love and patience.

I trust in my ability to nurture and guide my children, knowing that I am enough just as I am.

Each day, I choose to approach challenges with grace and to celebrate the joy in every moment.

Release Prayer:

Dear God,

Thank you for the gift of motherhood and the precious opportunity to nurture my children.

I ask for your guidance as I navigate the challenges and joys of parenting.

Please help me to be patient and present, to cherish the moments of connection, and to learn from every experience.

May I cultivate a loving environment where my children can thrive, and may I always remember that I am doing my best.

In moments of doubt, please remind me of your unwavering support. In Jesus' name, I pray, Amen.

Day Twenty-Two

Setting Healthy Boundaries

Boundaries safeguard peace and purpose. However, setting boundaries becomes an act of self-respect and a key part of healthy relationships. Boundaries show where we end and others begin, providing clarity about our needs, values, and limits. They are not barriers that block connection, but bridges that promote mutual understanding and respect. By respecting our boundaries and those of others, we create space for growth, trust, and honest communication.

As I reflect on a time when I lacked boundaries and it led to burnout and pain, I realize it was when I used not to tell people no. I would always come to their rescue or be there for them every time they needed me. I was everything for everyone, but then God allowed me to see it differently. They were never available for me; they had every excuse in the book or just didn't bother to care. I mean, Keyerra has been the ATM, the listening ear, the shopping partner, and more, but when I was in and out of the hospital or on bed rest, I saw who truly cared about me.

I wasn't expecting people to stop what they were doing, but I did at least expect a call, or visit. I did expect to be asked how I was doing, or if I needed anything. It means a lot when someone is going through something, they just want to know someone cares. But in that time of trouble, God was there, closer than any friend or brother. My breakthrough moment came when I decided to set a firm boundary and I had enough from my family. I decided I can't be nothing else to anyone else. I must protect my heart, and I need to focus on myself. I was literally fed up because if you ask for quality TIME from your family and they choose not to care or even set aside time, then, "'so be it". I want someone to cherish me while I'm still alive and not when I'm dead and gone. I feel you should'nt have to tell people to be present in your life and that it should come naturally.

But I honestly can say I'm okay with being the black sheep or people acting like I don't exist because it's your problem and your loss. The process of setting boundaries can feel uncomfortable at first, especially for those used to putting others first. Healthy boundaries allow us to say "no" without guilt and "yes" with purpose. As well, the process of setting boundaries can feel uncomfortable at first, especially for those used to putting others first. Still, each occurence is a statement of self-worth and a gentle reminder that our time, energy, and well-being are important.

It's important to understand that there is a significant difference between building walls and setting boundaries. Walls are rigid barriers we put up to keep others out, often in response to hurt or fear. They shut down opportunities for connection and healing, isolating us from relationships and experiences that could nurture our growth. Boundaries, on the other hand, are flexible and intentional; they do not block people out but instead define the healthy limits within which relationships can flourish. While walls are built out of self-protection and lead to emotional distance, boundaries are established from a place of self-respect and foster openness, mutual respect, and understanding.

In practice, walls might look like refusing to share your feelings, withdrawing completely when hurt, or never allowing others to get close. Boundaries, however, involve communicating your needs clearly and compassionately, saying "no" when necessary, and allowing space for both yourself and others to be authentic. Choosing boundaries over walls helps us maintain healthy connections while still honoring our own well-being.

As we learn to express our boundaries with compassion, we set an example of self-care for those around us. In turn, we foster deeper, more genuine connections where both people feel seen, heard, and appreciated. Over time, boundaries become an act of love, not just for us but also for those we share our journey with.

Scripture:

"Above all else, guard your heart, for everything you do flows from it." Proverbs 4:23 (NIV)

"Let your 'yes' be yes, and your 'no' be no. Matthew 5:37

Reflection/Journal:

"Where do I need stronger boundaries?"

Affirmations:

I am worthy of healthy boundaries that honor my needs and well-being.

Each day, I choose to communicate my limits with confidence and respect.

I embrace the freedom that comes from setting boundaries and protecting my energy.

Release Prayer:

Dear God,

I ask for your guidance as I learn to set
healthy boundaries in my life.

Please help me to recognize my worth and
the importance of my needs.

Grant me the strength to communicate my limits clearly and kindly, and the courage to stand firm in these decisions.

May I find peace in the protection of my heart and spirit, trusting that by setting boundaries, I create a space for growth and healing.

Thank you for your constant support as I navigate this journey. In Jesus' name, I pray, Amen.

May there be a balance to every part of life.

Day Twenty-Three

The Sound of Healing

Healing often has a sound of prayer, worship, laughter, release. Healing is rarely a silent process. More often, its language is written in notes and rhythms, in the hush between breaths or the resonance of a favorite song echoing across memory. Sound, in its infinite forms, has the uncanny power to reach places within us untouched by words. Where pain has taken root or sorrow lingers, music and gentle tones become balm, softening sharp edges, coaxing out hope, and reminding us that healing is not a linear path but a winding melody.

Amidst life's uncertainties, the act of listening...truly listening becomes a doorway to presence. The world's chaos can dissolve in the vibrato of a voice, the whisper of wind through leaves, or the steady comfort of a heartbeat nearby. Sometimes, the most profound shifts occur not in grand gestures but in the quiet moments when we allow ourselves to be cradled by the sounds around us.

A song that carried me through healing is called, "It's In The Room" by Jason Nelson. I would play it several times a day and just cry because the words spoke to vivid to my situation. My prayers to the father made me feel peace when I was having a bad day and in so much pain where I had been up longer than 48 hours. I would wrap myself up and just fall to my knees and pray.

For parents, caregivers, and individuals alike, intentionally welcoming healing sounds into daily routines can transform the atmosphere of a home and the cadence of a heart. A lullaby at bedtime, the shared laughter of loved ones, or the ritual of singing together after a long day. Each becomes a thread in the fabric of recovery and renewal. Sound, in these moments, becomes both anchor and sail: grounding us in the present and carrying us toward new horizons of well-being.

As we attune our lives to the healing qualities of sound, we come to recognize that our stories are interwoven with songs of resilience, sorrow, and celebration. Each note, each silence, offers a chance to begin again and as a gentle reminder that in listening, we find not only solace, but also the courage to move forward.

Music and sound significantly influence our emotional, mental, and physical health. They can trigger feelings of joy, nostalgia, and even healing, serving as powerful tools to improve our everyday lives.

Emotional Impact: Music has the power to connect with our emotions, often helping us process feelings that are hard to express. Whether it's the uplifting notes of a favorite song or the calming melodies of relaxing music, sound can lift our mood and offer comfort during difficult times.

Mental Clarity: Certain types of music, especially instrumental or ambient sounds, can boost concentration and cognitive function. Many people find that listening to music while working or studying helps them stay focused and be more productive.

Physical Healing: Sound therapy is increasingly recognized for its healing effects on the body. Frequencies from specific sound waves can encourage relaxation, lower stress, and even ease pain. Music therapy has been shown to support recovery from various conditions, boosting overall healing.

Social Connection: Music often brings people together, fostering bonds through shared experiences. experiences and emotions. Singing in groups or attending concerts fosters a sense of belonging and community, which are essential for emotional health.

Spiritual Connection: For many people, music serves as a way to connect with the divine or explore their personal spirituality. Anointed music can inspire feelings of peace and reflection, helping to deepen our spiritual journeys.

A moment I can remember being in worship at church and the worship was going on but me and God were in our own moment it shifted my atmosphere completely I remember just bowing down where I was and just letting go in his presence. The sound of laughter is very good healing marker because I feel that laughter is great for the soul.

Tears are also great for healing because it's a release and it reminds me of the scripture Ecclesiastes 3:4 where it states "For everything there is a season, and a time for every matter under heaven: a time to weep, a time to laugh; a time to mourn, and a time to dance."

Scripture:
You turned my mourning into dancing. Psalm 30:11

Reflection/Journal:
"What sounds bring me healing and peace?"

Affirmations:

I embrace the power of music and sound
to uplift, heal, and inspire me.

I allow melodies to bring joy and tranquility into my life.

With each note, I am reminded of my strength and
ability to connect with others and myself.

Release Prayer:

Dear God,

I thank you for the gift of music and sound in
my life. Please help me to be open to the healing
power of melodies and rhythms.

As I navigate my journey, may I find comfort and
joy through the notes that surround me.

Help me to share this gift with others, creating
spaces for connection and encouragement.

In moments of despair, remind me to turn to
the music that uplifts my spirit. Amen.

Day Twenty-Four

The Gifts of Gratitude

Gratitude multiplies joy and healing. As gratitude became my lifeline, I begin to see the beauty in observing what I did have. Although, there was a season when it wasn't just about virtue; it was about survival. Not because everything was good, but because everything hurt. I didn't give thanks because life felt easy; I gave thanks because it was the only way to keep my heart from collapsing under the weight of disappointment, grief, and unanswered prayers.

I remember waking up with more questions than strength. But instead of rehearsing my pain, I started whispering small praises: "God, Thank you for breath." "Thank you for keeping me when I didn't want to be kept." "Thank you that even though I don't understand, you are still here." I wasn't thanking God for the pain…I was thanking Him through it. And something shifted. Gratitude didn't change my situation overnight, but it changed me. It quieted my fear. It softened my bitterness. It reminded me that even in the valley, God was still providing manna and little mercies that were easy to miss unless I chose to see them.

Philippians 4:6-7 says, "In everything, by prayer and supplication, with thanksgiving, let your requests be made known to God, and the peace of God… will guard your hearts and minds." I used to think peace came after the miracle. But I learned peace comes after gratitude. So, if you're going through a tough season right now, don't wait for everything to make sense before you give thanks. Start small, start trembling, start tired if you have to, but just start. Because gratitude doesn't deny reality but it declares that even in it, God is still worthy.

Research shows that music can reduce stress hormones, boost mood, and even support the body's natural healing. Whether by singing, playing an instrument, or simply listening with focus, music provides a route to release and renewal. It reminds us that we aren't alone in our feelings; that someone, somewhere, has expressed feelings we may find hard to name. Incorporating music into daily life—such as morning melodies that mark new beginnings, peaceful soundscapes for reflection, or lively rhythms for celebration—creates moments of healing that spread outward. Even in silence, the echo of a favorite song can provide comfort, grounding us amid life's uncertainties. The act of choosing what we listen to becomes a gentle form of self-care, an opportunity to shape our inner world with sounds that uplift, inspire, and restore.

A small blessing I have learned to appreciate deeply is that I used to overlook the quiet moments and the sound of my own breath, the warmth of sunlight coming through the window, the ability to get out of bed without assistance. But life has a way of slowing you down to show you what truly matters. One of the greatest blessings I've learned to appreciate is simply having strength for the day. Not extraordinary strength, just enough to get dressed, enough to try again, enough to say "Lord, I'm still here another day." That 'enough' has become one of my greatest blessings.

As I reflect on a moment when practicing gratitude shifted my mood, it was a few months ago. It was a day when I had been to several doctor appointments and physical therapy. That day, everything felt heavy; my thoughts were loud, my spirit was restless, and frustration was winning. In that moment, I made myself pause and say out loud, "Thank you, God, that I still have breath in my body and the activity of my limbs. Thank you that this feeling is temporary. Thank you that you're giving me the strength I need to keep going." Those simple words didn't change my situation, but they changed my posture. Gratitude didn't erase the problem, but it reminded me I wasn't facing it alone, and suddenly, I felt lighter.

Scripture:

"Give thanks in all circumstances; for this is the will of God in Christ Jesus for you." 1 Thessalonians 5:18 (ESV)

Reflection/ Journal:

What am I thankful for in this season?

Affirmations:

I am grateful for the abundance in my life. I choose to focus on the blessings that surround me, cultivating a heart full of thankfulness. Each day, I celebrate the small joys that bring me peace and happiness.

Release Prayer:

Dear God,

Thank you for the countless blessings that fill my life, both big and small.

Help me to cultivate a heart of gratitude, even in challenging times.

Remind me to see the beauty in every moment and to appreciate the people and experiences that bring joy to my journey.

As I release negativity and embrace positivity, guide me to share this gratitude with others. May my heart overflow with thankfulness and love. In Jesus' name, I pray, Amen.

By adopting these practices, gratitude can serve as a transformative force in our lives, promoting positivity and helping us navigate challenges with a hopeful heart.

Day Twenty-Five

Embracing Authenticity and the Journey of Self-Discovery

True freedom comes from being yourself. There was a moment when I finally stopped pretending, and it came on a day when the weight of who I was pretending to be became heavier than the fear of who I really was. That moment was broken, damaged, and heartbroken. I was exhausted from shrinking myself to make others comfortable, exhausted from smiling when my soul was weary, exhausted from pretending to be strong instead of healing. The moment I chose authenticity over approval, something shifted. I didn't announce it. I didn't wait for permission from others. I simply exhaled… and let the masks fall.

I stopped apologizing for my voice.

I stopped dimming my light to blend in.

I stopped calling survival "strength" and finally started calling it what it was -exhaustion.

And in that quiet, liberating moment, I met me- the women I had buried beneath expectations and silence. I didn't become a new person. I returned to myself. The significance of living an authentic life. Opting to be honest and open as the basis for healing and building connection.

Embracing authenticity means letting our true selves shine, even when it feels risky or uncomfortable. It takes gentle courage to acknowledge our hopes, fears, and imperfections without judgment or pretense. As we allow ourselves to be authentic, we open the door to deeper relationships and a sense of freedom that comes from no longer hiding behind masks. In this space, healing can take root, and self-acceptance grows into self-love.

Day Twenty-Five ends with an invitation to move beyond the mask of expectation and embrace the raw honesty of being your true self. In this space of authenticity, transformation begins to take shape. It may happen gently, sometimes almost unnoticeably, but always with significant effects on the heart and soul.

As we practice living authentically, we uncover new layers of freedom. Revealing who we truly are, even in small ways, can open the door to acceptance, forgiveness, and deeper connection with others. Vulnerability becomes less a risk and more a source of strength, helping us build relationships based on truth rather than pretense.

With each step toward embracing our story, we open space for compassion toward ourselves and those around us. Healing becomes not just an individual pursuit but a shared journey, where our authenticity acts as a beacon for others to follow. In this atmosphere of acceptance, the seeds of self-discovery are quietly planted, setting the stage for the next chapter: the deliberate and wondrous journey inward.

For a long time, I didn't realize how much of my life was a performance. I was who people needed me to be—strong when I was hurting, polite when I was angry, present even when I was empty. I wore so many versions of myself that I forgot which one was truly mine.But the moment I started choosing authenticity over approval, everything shifted.Some relationships fell silent when I stopped overextending myself. Not because I was rude...but because I finally learned how to say, "That's not okay," or "I can't keep pouring from an empty cup." And yes, it hurt to see people walk away—but it also showed me who truly loved me and not just what I could do for them.

Authenticity also changed how I walk with God. I used to pray polished prayers....the kind that sound holy but don't say anything. One day I got tired and said, "God, I'm not okay." And I swear that's when I finally felt Him the most. Not in the pretending—but in the breaking. I realized God doesn't bless masks. He heals hearts. And the biggest change was my self-perception. I stopped introducing myself to the world as who I should be and started honoring who I actually am. I'm no longer afraid to be too quiet, too deep, too opinionated, too emotional, too real. The parts I used to hide became the parts that set me free. Authenticity didn't simplify my life but it made it more genuine. And I'd choose genuine over perfect any day. Being your authentic self won't be easy.

One of the first challenges was the fear of rejection. I worried that people wouldn't accept the real me and that my scars, struggles, and raw emotions would push them away. And honestly, some did, because remember, people don't like genuine folks who don't put on a front for others. That hurt, but it also revealed who truly belonged in my life.

Another challenge was breaking old habits. For years, I masked my pain, doubts, and even my joy to fit in or be acceptable. That was settling for less than my worth. Choosing honesty meant unlearning patterns I'd lived by for decades. It was uncomfortable and sometimes lonely, but necessary. I also faced misunderstanding; people misinterpreted my boundaries or honesty as coldness or pride. They didn't always see the courage it took to stop performing and start speaking the truth.

Lastly, I wrestled with self-doubt. I often asked myself: Am I too much? Not enough? Will God really use me as I am? Learning to lean on Him for validation instead of the world became essential. Through it all, I realized the hardest part of authenticity isn't the world- it's trusting yourself and God enough to show up fully, even when it's uncomfortable. And every step forward has been worth it.

Scripture:

I praise you because I am fearfully and wonderfully made; your works are wonderful; I know that full well." Psalm 139:14 (NIV)

Reflection/ Journal:

Where have I been pretending instead of being authentic

Affirmations:

"I embrace the journey of self-discovery with courage and grace.

I am open to learn from my experiences, trusting that each step I take brings me closer to my true self.

My past does not define me; instead, it shapes me into the resilient person I am becoming.

I honor my journey and believe in the beauty of my unfolding."

Release Prayer:

Dear God, I come before You with an open heart, seeking clarity and direction on my journey of self-discovery.

I release any fears, doubts, or negative beliefs that have held me back from embracing my true identity.

Guide me as I navigate this path, helping me to uncover the talents, passions, and purpose you have instilled in me.

May I find healing in my past, strength in my present,

and hope for my future. I trust in Your plans for me and surrender to Your wisdom. Amen.

Day Twenty-Six

The Journey of Self-Discovery: Embracing Pain, Purpose, and Stillness

Pain can reveal purpose if we take the time to reflect. "In a rare moment of stillness, when the world paused around me, clarity washed over my mind and purpose stirred in my heart. It was as if God whispered the next steps of my journey, and suddenly the path forward was no longer uncertain- it was illuminated with intention and peace."

Every scar I carry tells a story of pain, endurance, and growth. At first, I saw them as reminders of what I survived- but over time, I realized they were signposts pointing toward my calling. Each scar shaped my empathy, my strength, and my purpose, guiding me to walk boldly into the path I was meant to fulfill. In the quiet, I learned that silence isn't empty instead it's full of answers. Solitude taught me that not every battle needs movement; some victories are won in stillness. When I stopped forcing solutions and simply sat with my thoughts, I discovered that peace had been speaking the whole time. I was just too loud to hear it. Reflection revealed that clarity doesn't always come through action but through surrender.

During moments of pain, we often lose the distractions that obscure our view. This clarity helps us identify our passions, as we're no longer willing to accept a life without meaning. The struggle can spark a fire inside us, motivating us to chase what we've always longed for but may have previously overlooked. Furthermore, pain can foster empathy and understanding, prompting us to seek purpose beyond ourselves. Those who have faced significant adversity often feel a strong desire to help others experiencing similar challenges. This connection can lead to advocacy, creative expression, or acts of service, channeling the energy from pain into meaningful actions.

Ultimately, navigating through pain can empower us to discover our true selves. It encourages us to accept our perceived flaws and scars, turning them into symbols of resilience and strength. This awakening can help us gain a clearer understanding of our unique purpose, inspiring us to live fully and passionately, with a dedication to making the world better through our experiences. By embracing our pain, we build a foundation for a life filled with purpose and deep passion.

In the rush toward healing and transformation, God's invitation emerges: to rest in the gentle embrace of stillness. This quiet pause is not an absence of movement, but rather a space that allows wisdom and insight to surface quietly. Within the silence, burdens lighten, and self-compassion deepens. Stillness shows us that it is not always through striving that we find wholeness, but by allowing ourselves to be and to be present, open, and receptive to grace.

During these moments, the heart learns a new language: gratitude for each breath, each heartbeat, and every small step forward. Stillness becomes a victory itself, a sign of the courage required to pause amid the storm, to acknowledge both the pain and the promise of the present. With this view, we get ready to celebrate the subtle yet meaningful milestones on our journey.

Finding Purpose Through Stillness and Reflection

In a world that celebrates constant movement, it's easy to think that purpose is found in hustle, noise, and nonstop striving. But what if the very answer we're seeking can only be heard in the quiet? Stillness is not laziness, instead it's deliberate awareness. Reflection is not obsessing over the past and it's extracting wisdom from it.

If you want to discover your purpose, try this process:
Create Silence: Turn off the noise—phones, people, distractions. Your mind cannot recognize direction when it's constantly flooded with voices other than your own and God's. Purpose is often whispered, not shouted.

Ask Yourself More Thoughtful Questions:

Instead of asking, "What am I supposed to do with my life?" consider asking this instead:
- What experiences have influenced me the most?
- What weighs heavily on me? What makes me cry or sparks my passion?
- What comes naturally to me that helps others?

Your past pain often shows your future purpose.

3. Revisit Your Scars, Not as Wounds, but instead as clues:

Reflection helps you stop viewing your struggles as random. Look back intentionally and ask:
- What did that season teach me?
- Who can I help now because of what I learned?

What once hurt you might now be your biggest strength.

Listen for God's Echo:

Purpose is often confirmed through recurring themes—scriptures, conversations, ideas that keep reappearing. Stillness helps you notice patterns you might miss when distracted.

Proceed Carefully, Yet Obediently:

Clarity doesn't always happen all at once. Sometimes God shows direction step by step. Reflection gives you the courage to move forward without needing the whole map. Stillness isn't the lack of progress—it's where purpose is born.

Scripture:
"He heals the brokenhearted and binds up their wounds." Psalm 147:3:

Reflection/ Journal:
"What am I learning about myself through my scars?"

Affirmations:
I embrace my scars as symbols of my strength and resilience.

Each day, I choose to see my past experiences as opportunities for growth and learning.

I am empowered to reclaim my story and create a beautiful narrative of healing and transformation.

Release Prayer:
Dear God,

I come to you with an open heart, ready to acknowledge my scars and the journey I have traveled.

Help me see my experiences not as burdens but as invaluable lessons that contribute to my growth.

Please grant me the strength to share my story with others, fostering connection and empathy.

As I embrace my imperfections and the beauty of my journey, remind me that I am wonderfully made in your image.

Thank you for your healing presence and for guiding me as I continue to transform my narrative. In Jesus' name, I pray, Amen.

Day Twenty-Seven

Celebrating Small Victories

Healing is a journey made up of small victories. While pursuing healing and growth, it's easy to overlook the simple power of just being present. Taking time to honor the current moment helps strengthen our connection to ourselves and the world around us. Mindfulness encourages us to pause, breathe, and recognize both challenges and joys that shape our path. By remaining rooted in the present, we gain clarity and resilience, finding peace even amid change.

Sometimes, it's not the mountains that show God's faithfulness it's the pebbles. I remember a day when I didn't get the breakthrough I prayed for... but I received something small. Maybe it was waking up without anxiety gripping my chest. Maybe it was having just enough gas to get to work. Maybe it was the bill that somehow got paid when the math didn't make sense. To anyone else, it wouldn't look like a miracle. But to me, it was proof that God saw me.

That small victory changed my mindset from "God, are you even listening?" to "Maybe He's been working behind the scenes all along." That's the thing about little wins: They whisper before the big blessings shout, they soften your heart before the breakthrough arrives, and they grow gratitude before God releases greater.

I want to challenge you before the day ends: pause and thank God for one small victory. It may seem insignificant but watch how it expands your faith. This is how small wins kept me going. I used to think progress only counted when it was big—like a promotion, full healing, or reaching a goal. But somewhere along the journey, I realized something powerful: the small wins were what kept me alive during the process. There were days I didn't conquer the mountain...I just lay there because I couldn't get out of bed. I couldn't stay stuck; I had to push myself to take one step. I didn't feel overflowing with joy... I just whispered "God, help me" instead of giving up. And you know what? Every time I acknowledged a tiny win, my spirit got stronger. Celebrating a good day gave me hope for the next. Thanking God for "just enough" reminded me he was still providing. Recognizing progress, no matter how small, kept me from falling back into discouragement. I stopped waiting to arrive to feel proud. I started praising God for every inch of progress. Because momentum is built one small victory at a time.

A day when I felt progress even if it wasn't perfect, remember a day when everything didn't go as planned. I woke up with a long to-do list and big expectations, but by evening, I had only accomplished a portion of it. Normally, I would've been frustrated with myself disappointed that I hadn't done enough. But that day felt different. Instead of being hard on myself, I paused and acknowledged the small steps I did take. No, it wasn't perfect, and I still had loose ends and incomplete tasks but for once I chose to see progress instead of failure.

I realized that healing, growth, and becoming who God called me to be wasn't about perfection- it was about consistency. It was about showing up, even if I didn't have it all together. That day reminded me that I am not where I used to be. I may not be at the finish line yet, but Im moving forward and that's worth celebrating. Progress is still progress, even when its imperfect. I thank God for the grace to keep going.

If there's one thing I've learned, it's this: we don't just wake up healed, disciplined, confident, or successful. We become—one small step at a time. That's why I started intentionally tracking my progress instead of only measuring my perfection.

Here's what helped me, and maybe it will help you too:

How to Track and Celebrate Incremental Progress:
- Write down your "wins" at the end of each day — Not just the big ones. If you got out of bed when you didn't feel like it, that counts. If you prayed instead of panicked, that's growth. If you said "no" to something that drained you, that's strength.
- Compare yourself to who you were, not who you want to be — It's easy to feel behind when you're looking at the finish line. Instead, glance back at how far you've already come. You're further than you think.
- Create visual proof of progress — Use a journal, checklist, habit tracker, or even voice memos. Seeing your growth over time builds motivation.
- Celebrate out loud—even if it feels small — You don't have to wait for a graduation moment to clap for yourself. Whisper "I'm proud of me" after each step. Heaven celebrates progress—we should too.
- Turn setbacks into data, not defeat — If you slipped, don't shame yourself. Ask, what can I learn from this? Forward motion is still forward, even when it's messy.

The truth is that transformation isn't always loud. Sometimes it's quiet discipline. Sometimes it's choosing peace. Sometimes it's getting back up. So today, instead of asking "Did I do it perfectly?" ask, "Did I move?" If the answer is yes, then you're already winning.

Scripture:

Do not despise small beginnings. Zechariah 4:10

Reflection/ Journal:
What small victories can I celebrate today?

Affirmations:
I thank God for every small victory because even tiny steps move me forward.

I choose to see progress, not perfection, knowing momentum is built one small win at a time.

I am proud of my growth today, even if it didn't look perfect and because grace counts as progress.

Release Prayer:
Dear God,

As I begin this journey of healing, I ask for your strength and wisdom. Please help me to see my scars as symbols of my survival and resilience.

Allow me to shift my perspective from one of victimhood to one of empowerment, embracing the lessons from my experiences.

Please give me the courage to share my story, building connections with others who may need hope and understanding.

Remind me that you beautifully make me, and my scars tell the unique story of your grace in my life.

Thank you for guiding me through this process of healing and growth. In Jesus' name, I pray, Amen.

Day Twenty-Eight

The Journey of Forgiveness and Healing

Forgiveness frees you from the chains of the past. It begins within. Be gentle with yourself on this journey. Recognize that healing takes time, and self-compassion is essential as you navigate your feelings. There was a person I struggled to forgive - not because what they did was unforgivable, but because the pain they caused kept replaying in my mind like a movie, I had seen several times. I told myself I had moved on, but every time their name came up, or a certain memory resurfaced, my chest tightened. I couldn't understand why I was still emotionally chained to something I claimed to be "over."

I wanted justice, I wanted an apology, I wanted them to understand just how deeply their actions had affected me. But one day, I realized I was giving them power over my peace. I was still allowing what happened to dictate how I felt. That's when I understood forgiveness isn't about letting them off the hook. It's about freeing me. It's choosing to stop letting that situation define me. It's closing the door, not because the story was fair, but because I refuse to let it write any more chapters of my life.

I won't pretend it was easy. Forgiveness requires "process". Some days I felt healed, other days I felt angry all over again. But every time I chose to release over resentment, I felt a layer of weight lift off me. I didn't forgive them because they asked. I forgave because I deserved peace. For the longest time, I believed forgiveness was something I gave to others and that it was a gift they had to earn. But I didn't realize forgiveness was actually something I needed to give myself. Not because what happened was okay, but because carrying the weight of anger was slowly draining me. I thought holding onto the pain protected me, but in reality, it was poisoning me.

The moment I chose forgiveness even before I felt it noticed something shift inside me. My heart softened. My mind quieted. I stopped rehearsing old conversations and started imagining a future that wasn't chained to what hurt me. Forgiveness didn't erase the memory, but it removed the sting. It allowed me to look back without bleeding. It helped me separate what was done to me from who I was becoming. It turned my wounds into wisdom instead of walls.

Most importantly, forgiveness made room for healing. My prayers changed. Instead of "God, fix them," it became "God, free me." Instead of anger, I felt gratitude for every lessonlearned, strength discovered, and growth I never would've found without that pain.Forgiveness didn't just change my situation. It changed me. It took me from victim to victor. From bitter to better. From broken to becoming. For a long time, I thought bitterness was my shield. It made me feel in control. I thought if I stayed guarded, I couldn't be hurt again. But what I didn't realize was that bitterness wasn't protecting me…it was imprisoning me. The more I held onto it, the heavier my spirit became. Smiles were forced. Joy was temporary.

Even the good moments felt dull because somewhere deep inside, I was still replaying pain.When I finally chose grace it was not because they deserved it, but because I needed it. I began to see life differently. Here are the lessons forgiveness taught me:

Lessons Learned from Choosing Grace Over Bitterness
- Grace isn't about pretending it didn't hurt — it's

- choosing not to live wounded.
- Bitterness keeps you stuck in a moment that already passed. Grace lets you move forward.
- Sometimes the person who needs the most grace is you.
- Releasing someone doesn't make you weak — it proves how strong you've become.
- Peace feels better than being right.
- Grace turns pain into purpose — bitterness only repeats the pain.
- God can heal what you hand over, not what you keep holding onto.

Choosing grace didn't change the past, but it changed me.It didn't fix everything around me, but it fixed something within me. And now, instead of carrying bitterness, I carry wisdom, and that's a much lighter load.

Scriptures:

Forgive as the Lord forgave you. Colossians 3:13

But if you do not forgive others thier sins, your father will not forgive your sins. Matthew 6:15

For I will restore health to you, and your wounds I will heal, says the Lord. Jeremiah 30:17

These scriptures remind us of the power of forgiveness and healing, encouraging us to extend grace to ourselves and others.

Reflection/Journal:

"Who do I need to forgive, including myself?"

Affirmations:

I am open to the healing power of forgiveness.

Each day, I choose to let go of resentment and embrace peace.

I recognize my worthiness and allow love and understanding to guide my heart.

Release Prayer:

Dear God,

Finally, recognize that forgiveness leads to healing. Embrace this new sense of peace and let it inspire growth.

As you release resentments, welcome the opportunities for joy, love, and fulfillment that come into your life.

Forgiveness is a powerful tool that unlocks the door to personal healing and emotional well-being.

By embracing this road, you open yourself up to a life filled with hope, connection, and profound inner peace.

Day Twenty-Nine

Resilient on Purpose: The Beauty of the Bounce Back

Resilience is a learned practice that grows over time. Resilience isn't something we're born with; it's developed through our experiences. It's the quiet strength that helps us get up one more time than we fall, the whisper encouraging us to keep going when life feels overwhelming. Cultivating resilience doesn't mean ignoring hardship or pretending pain isn't there; it means embracing it. Instead, it invites us to face our struggles with awareness, compassion, and a strong belief in our ability to heal.

There came a point in my life when it felt like I was living in a loop of loss. I'd try to get back up, and life would shove me down again. A little progress. Then another diagnosis. A moment of joy. Then another heartbreak. I got so familiar with disappointment that I stopped expecting things to work out. One morning, I sat on the edge of my bed, tired, not physically, but soul tired. Tired of praying bold prayers with trembling faith. Tired of starting over. Tired of pretending strength while silently breaking. I remember whispering, "Lord, I don't mind fighting…I just need You to give me the strength to swing." That prayer didn't magically change my situation although, it did change me.

I used to think resilience meant being naturally strong, being the girl who could take every hit and keep smiling. But I learned resilience is less about natural strength and more about learned endurance. It didn't come from one breakthrough moment but it came from daily choices: I spoke life over myself when my feelings spoke defeat. Some mornings I didn't feel like a warrior, so I talked to myself like one. "You will recover. You will heal. You will see goodness again."I didn't wait to 'feel ready' to live again. I praised God with shaky hands. I moved forward with trembling knees. Sometimes resilience is just showing up when quitting feels easier. I stopped isolating and starting reaching out. There's a lie that tells us asking for help makes us weak. The truth? It makes us human. And humans are designed to survive in community, not isolation.

The Two people Who Taught Me How to Stand Again

My husband and daughter don't even realize it, but they were my mirrors of resilience. My husband stood beside me through storms that would have sent others running. Not because everything was easy, but because his love was anchored. Watching him carry faith through fire made me want to rise with him- not leave him carrying the weight alone. And my daughter just looking at her reminded me that giving up was not an option. She made me fight differently not just for myself, but for the version of me she would one day look up to. They taught me that resilience isn't always loud. Sometimes it's choosing to breathe through the pain so you can live long enough to see the promise.

The bounceback I need didn't happen overnight. Instead, it took time and I rose in layers. Slowly emerging until I realizing I was out of what I had been in. Resilience isn't about never falling, yet it's about refusing to stay down. My scars don't just tell stories of what hurt me. They tell stories of every comeback I survived.

Scripture:

Consider it pure joy, my brothers and sisters, whenever you

face trials of many kinds, because you know that the testing of your faith produces perseverance." James 1:2-3 (NIV)

Reflection/Journal:

What strengthens my resilience?

Affirmations:

I embrace life's challenges as opportunities for growth and resilience.

I recognize that through trials, I am strengthened and equipped to face whatever comes my way.

I choose to persevere with faith, knowing that each setback is a setup for a comeback.

I am resilient, capable, and worthy of overcoming obstacles.

Release Prayer:

Dear God,

Help me cultivate resilience in the face of trials.

Teach me to find joy in challenges and to see them as valuable lessons. Please grant me the strength to persevere when I encounter difficulties and the wisdom to learn and grow from each experience.

Surround me with Your peace and support as I navigate life's journeys. In Jesus' name, I pray, Amen.

Embrace the resilience within you, trusting that it will carry you through every storm.

Day Thirty

Looking Toward the Future

Vision, hope, and future steps beyond healing. As the healing journey progresses, the horizon shines with promise. Looking ahead is more than just hope, instead it's a deliberate act of shaping what comes next. Healing doesn't merely restore what was lost; it opens new paths, inspiring us to set intentions that honor both our scars and our dreams. There was a time when I honestly didn't believe I would ever feel whole again. My body carried scars, but my heart bore deeper ones—rejection, loss, disappointment, unanswered prayers. I had learned how to function while broken, but deep down, I didn't know if true healing was ever going to be my reality.

Then one night, God met me in my sleep. I had a dream where I saw me and it was not the me that was hurting, not the me that was pretending to be okay, but a healed me. I was standing confidently in front of people, sharing my story with no shame, no trembling voice, no hidden pain. I was smiling. I was free. And people listening were being restored because of my testimony. I woke up with tears streaming down my face and not from grief but from hope. For the first time, I believed healing wasn't just possible, but it was promised. Ever since that dream, I've been taking intentional steps and not just to survive but to live again.

- I speak even when I feel nervous, because my story isn't just mine—it's someone else's survival guide.

- I protect my peace without apologizing, because I finally understand that boundaries are holy.
- I embrace joy without waiting for the "other shoe to drop," because I refuse to treat happiness like it's temporary.
- I honor my scars instead of hiding them, because they don't make me damaged—they make me evidence.

One day, I caught myself laughing, really and it was not the polite kind. Not the "I'm okay" kind. It was the kind that comes from the soul. I stopped mid-laugh and realized…"I don't feel heavy anymore." That was it. That was my moment. Not when everything was perfect. Not when every prayer was answered. But when joy no longer felt foreign. If God could resurrect my heart, He can do it for anyone reading this. Healing didn't erase my scars but now, they testify louder than my pain ever did.

While we may be full of purpose and clarity, it is often not without challenges. So you to set goals that support your well-being: maybe you want to strengthen relationships, chase long-neglected passions, or enjoy small everyday moments that cultivate gratitude. Let your dreams be grounded in compassion for yourself, understanding that progress isn't about perfection but persistence.

Embrace the power of small, manageable steps. Each goal, no matter how minor, acts like a seed planted in fertile soil. Maybe your first vow is to speak kindly to yourself every morning or to share your story with someone who needs hope. Perhaps you choose to pursue a creative passion or forgive a wound you've long held onto. With every intention you set, you reaffirm your commitment to growth, resilience, and self-love.

Remember to revisit and renew your aspirations as you grow and change. The future isn't a fixed point but a living, breathing journey which shaped by your choices, courage, and willingness to heal. Allow yourself to dream boldly. Imagine a future where your scars are not burdens but wings: reminders of how far you've come and the endless possibilities still ahead. With each sunrise, let your goals illuminate your path. Dare to imagine a tomorrow where hope isn't just wished for, but actively built—one compassionate choice, one brave step at a time.

Scripture:

For I know the plans I have for you," declares the Lord, "plans to prosper you and not to harm you, plans to give you hope and a future." Jeremiah 29:11 (NIV)

Reflection/ Journal:

What goals have you set for yourself?

Affirmations:

I trust that my future is in God's hands, filled with hope and potential. I embrace the journey ahead with confidence, knowing that my dreams can align with His purpose for my life. I believe in my ability to create a bright future and acknowledge that fear will not dictate my path. I am ready to step into the opportunities that await me, embracing growth and transformation at every turn.

Release Prayer:

Dear God,

As I look toward the future, I seek your guidance and wisdom. Thank you for the promise that you have plans for my life, filled with hope and opportunity.

Help me release any anxieties or doubts I hold about what lies ahead. Grant me the courage to step forward with faith and an open heart, trusting that each day brings new possibilities.

May I remain steadfast in my journey, knowing
that You are with me every step of the way.

Surround me with Your grace and love as I navigate the future You have planned for me. In Jesus' name, I pray, Amen.

Embrace the future with optimism, recognizing that it is woven into the beautiful tapestry of God's plans for your life.

Day Thirty-One

Conclusion: Your Scars Tell a Story

Closure and empowerment are important because our scars are our testimony. Healing isn't a straight road or a goal reached quickly. It's a perfect picture of our moments, some victorious, others filled with longing with each shaping the story written on our skin and in our hearts. As you finish this book, remember that every step forward, no matter how small, shows your bravery. Your scars aren't signs of defeat but symbols of honor but also proof of battles fought, and wisdom gained.

There was a time when I tried to hide everything I had survived. I thought silence was strength and pretending was protection. But the truth is my pain didn't begin to heal until I stopped covering it. Looking back, I see a clear divide in my life: before healing and after surrender. I went from questioning God's love to experiencing it deeply in the darkest moments. I went from rejecting myself to learning how to speak gently to the girl in the mirror. I went from simply existing to discovering purpose within the very wounds that once shamed me.

My faith transformed when I realized that God did not just want to save my soul—He wanted to restore my story. My self-love deepened when I chose to stop treating survival as my identity. And my purpose became clear the moment I understood: my scars were never designed to silence me instead they were meant to testify. If you are reading this with trembling hands, holding back tears, wondering if healing is possible for you, then this is your sign that it is. You don't have to wait until you feel "ready" or "worthy." Healing doesn't ask for perfection it asks for permission. You have permission to feel, to confront and to begin again.

Your story isn't over it's just beginning so, I invite you to tell your truth, honor your scars, and walk boldly toward the life that still belongs to you. If my scars can speak, so can yours and trust me someone is waiting to hear them. My scars speak fear, pain, anger, sadness, gain, confidence, resilience, boldness, truth, choices, peace, survival, life, God's promises, and a profound beauty and love for myself that I never thought I would see.

Letter to My Younger Self

I want to start by saying something you may never have heard the way you needed it: I'm proud of you. Truly proud. Not for what you do, or what you achieve, or how strong you are when life demands more than it should from someone your age. I'm proud of you for simply surviving and for carrying the weight of a world you were never meant to carry and doing it with a heart that never hardened, even when it could have.

I know you've felt invisible at times. I know there were days when your own father seemed to see everyone else before you and when you were left wondering if your worth was measured only by your usefulness or how well you could endure. Those moments stung in ways that still echo. But, the truth is, his inability to see you does not define you. You are far more valuable than his recognition. You always have been. And I want you to carry that in your pocket like a small, unbreakable light to pull out when the darkness feels too heavy.

I remember how early you were forced to grow up. You carried responsibility that should have been shared, felt pressures that should have been softened with guidance and gentle hands. You learned lessons before your time and lessons about betrayal, about loss, about being let down by the people you trusted most. And yet, you never stopped believing in love. You never gave up on hope. That stubborn hope is part of the armor that has shaped the woman I am today. Never think your youthful resilience is weakness and it is the blueprint for your courage.

I know there were nights when your body betrayed you. The pain you've carried included the secret cramps, the fatigue, the endless tests, the disappointment of miscarriages and loss. And it was too much for anyone your age to carry alone. And yet, you carried it. You felt the ache in ways that nobody around you could understand, and for so long, you did it quietly, hiding it behind a smile. Baby girl, it is okay to acknowledge that pain, to let it break you for a moment, because it will also teach you the depth of your strength. There will come a day when your body and your scars become testimony, a living proof that survival is not a passive act..it is an art, a form of resistance, a declaration that your story matters.

I know your heart has been bruised in ways that feel permanent. Love, in its purest form, has seemed elusive, and many times you've wondered if you're too much or not enough. But here's a secret the future you know you are enough always. And the kind of love that truly sees you, the kind that chooses you over and over, will come. It may not look like what you imagine; it may not arrive when you expect it. But when it comes, you will recognize it not because it is perfect, but because it is patient, gentle, and unwavering in its commitment to you. Until then, learn to love yourself fiercely. Cherish yourself the way you have always longed to be cherished. The way your father could not show you, the way your early loves could not, the way the world sometimes fails to recognize and you can give that love to yourself. And that love will be the very thing that guides you when everyone else falls short.

I know that rejection has been a shadow that follows you, sometimes quietly, sometimes in a way that makes it impossible to breathe. I know the sting of wanting someone to be proud of you. Especially your father, and feeling like your best was never enough. I want you to know that this rejection is not a reflection of your value. The world may not always see your brilliance, the people you love may not always acknowledge your worth, but the truth is, you are extraordinary. Your gifts, your compassion, your ability to persevere, all these are things that no amount of rejection can take from you. Let the disappointment of others shape your wisdom, not your self-worth.

You have been asked to forgive before you were ready. You have been asked to understand when your heart was raw. And sometimes, you may feel that forgiving means excusing, that understanding means condoning. But forgiveness is not about them instead it is about you. Every act of grace you extend to those who hurt you frees you. It frees your heart, your spirit, your body. I know this may sound impossible when the pain is fresh, when the betrayal cuts deep, but I promise you: the day you choose to release the bitterness, even a little, will feel like stepping out of a prison you didn't know you were trapped in. That freedom is yours to claim! Claim it often.

There will be moments of heartbreak that feel like endings and moments when your body fails, when a relationship crumbles, when your dreams seem to dissolve before your eyes. But I want you to hear this clearly: endings are not the whole story. Every loss, every ache, every tear you shed plants a seed in the soil of your future. Pain is not punishment; it is preparation. It is shaping you, molding you into someone who can withstand storms, someone who can comfort others with empathy, someone who can celebrate victories with a depth that only comes from having walked through valleys.

Your body, though it may frustrate you, will teach you patience and courage. There will be seasons of waiting and some that feel endless. There are seasons where answers will not come, where healing seems slow, where losses feel like they pile one upon the other. But I need you to trust this: your body, your spirit, your hear are all resilient beyond measure. You will learn to listen to yourself in ways that nobody else taught you. You will understand the value of your own voice, your own choices, your own boundaries. And in that, you will discover empowerment.

I know your heart longs to be seen, to be chosen, to be wanted. And sometimes that longing feels like a void that cannot be filled. Let me tell you something vital: the love you seek outwardly must first reside within you. You have to learn to be your own sanctuary, your own safe place. You have to embrace the little girl who cries in her room, the teenager who feels unseen, the young adult who wonders if she will ever be enough. Hold them close. Teach them kindness. Speak to them gently. Because the woman you will become is built upon the foundation of that self-compassion.

There will be days when you stumble and fall. Days when you question your purpose, your calling, your very existence. I want you to know that falling does not make you weak. In fact, it is the act of rising after each fall that forges the deepest courage. Do not be afraid of mistakes—they are signposts, not tombstones. Every misstep, every heartbreak, every failure carries a lesson that you will carry into your future victories. You will come to see that your scars are not signs of defeat—they are the proof of resilience, the evidence of battles fought and survived. They are your badges of honor. Wear them proudly.

And, I need you to hear this: your journey will touch others in ways you cannot yet imagine. Your pain will become a bridge for someone else's healing. Your strength will be a light for those who stumble in darkness. Your compassion will be a balm for hearts that ache in silence. Every trial you endure, every tear you shed, every moment you have questioned your worth. Everything that happened…all of it has purpose beyond what you can see right now. You are being shaped to not only survive, but to lead, to inspire, to heal.

There will come a day when you look back and marvel at how far you've come. You will see that the battles you thought were defeating you were, in fact, refining you. You will realize that the love you longed for, the recognition you craved, the peace you sought….they were never truly missing. They were always within you, waiting for you to claim them. And when that day comes, you will smile at your younger self, not with judgment, not with impatience, but with profound understanding and tenderness. You will finally tell her, "You did it. You made it. You are everything you were created to be."

I want you to take this letter and tuck it somewhere close, somewhere you can reach when the weight feels too heavy. Read it when you feel unseen. Read it when your body aches. Read it when love seems out of reach. Let these words wrap around you like a warm embrace from someone who knows you intimately, someone who has walked through fire and come out shining. Because that person is me and that person has never stopped believing in you.

I cannot promise life will always be easy. I cannot promise that pain will vanish or that disappointments will cease. But I can promise that you will endure. You will rise. You will find joy in the places you least expect it. You will love fiercely, even when it hurts. You will be cherished by those who see the value in your heart. And most importantly, you will never, ever lose yourself.

So, my darling, hear me now: You are worthy. You are loved. You are capable of far more than you have ever imagined. You are a warrior—not because you are unbroken, but because you have chosen to rise every time life tried to bend you. Keep going. Keep believing. Keep holding on to that small, stubborn hope that has carried you this far. And when the world says otherwise, when rejection whispers lie in your ear, when your body aches and your heart trembles, return to these words. Let them remind you who you are. Let them remind you that even when the world failed you, you did not fail yourself.

Baby Girl, I see you. I love you. And I am endlessly proud of you. With all the tenderness and strength, I can muster.

Your Future Self

www.ingramcontent.com/pod-product-compliance
Lightning Source LLC
Chambersburg PA
CBHW070550170426
43201CB00012B/1794